Smart Client Architecture and Design Guide

patterns & practices

David Hill, Microsoft Corporation

Brenton Webster, Microsoft Corporation

Edward A. Jezierski, Microsoft Corporation

Srinath Vasireddy, Microsoft Corporation

Mo Al-Sabt, Microsoft Corporation

Blaine Wastell, Ascentium Corporation

Jonathan Rasmusson, ThoughtWorks

Paul Gale, ThoughtWorks

Paul Slater, Wadeware LLC

ISBN 0-7356-1853-4

Contents

Chapter 3
Getting Connected   39

Chapter 4
Occasionally Connected Smart Clients   51

Foreword

The Microsoft®.NET Framework and Windows Forms are a great platform for building smart client applications that combine all the power, flexibility, and great user experience of the rich client application model with the ease of deployment and stability of browser-based applications. The .NET Framework solves DLL versioning conflicts and simplifies deployment. Windows Forms has a powerful library of user interface components and an-easy-to use forms designer that combines the ease of use of the Microsoft Visual Basic® 6.0 programming model with the power and flexibility of the .NET Framework.

However, no matter how easy Windows Forms makes building your user interface, there are still numerous design challenges you will need to solve when building your smart client applications. What is the right deployment model for your application? How do you enable offline processing? What about data security? How do you keep the application responsive to the user when connecting over low bandwidth? What are the things you need to do to build an application that meets your users' performance expectations? The list goes on.

If you don't have a clear understanding of what these challenges are and what you need to do to address them early in your development cycle, trying to retrofit solutions later can be costly and painful. *Smart Client Architecture and Design Guide* helps you to figure out what the design challenges are and guides you toward the right solutions for your project. This is exactly the kind of information customers have been asking us for, so I'm excited to see this guide published.

Have fun building client applications again!

Mark Boulter
PM Technical Lead

Mark Boulter is a senior PM on the .NET Client team at Microsoft. Mark has worked on Windows Forms and related class libraries since joining Microsoft. Before joining Microsoft, Mark worked as a consultant for ParcPlace Systems in the UK helping customers build client-server and data analysis systems in Smalltalk. Prior to that, Mark spent more years than he is willing to admit at IBM in the UK working on a variety of projects including large scale client server systems, a CASE tool, a workflow engine, and order management systems. Mark's interests include listening to post punk industrial new wave and blues, reading pretty much anything he picks up, and herding cats.

1

Introduction

Welcome to the *Smart Client Architecture and Design Guide*. Smart client applications are a powerful alternative to thin client applications. They can provide users with a rich and responsive user interface, the ability to work offline, and a way to take advantage of local hardware and software resources. In addition, they can be designed to run on a broad spectrum of client devices, including desktop PCs, Tablet PCs, and handheld mobile devices such as Pocket PCs and Smartphones. Smart clients give users access to information and remote services within a powerful and intuitive client environment, and are an effective solution for flexible user-oriented applications and for increasing user productivity and satisfaction.

Smart client applications can be designed to combine the traditional benefits of a rich client application with the manageability benefits of a thin client application. However, to fully realize the benefits of a smart client application, you need to consider a number of architectural and design issues. This guide describes the architectural and design challenges you will face when designing and implementing a smart client application. It provides guidance on how to overcome these challenges, allowing you realize the benefits of a smart client application in as short a time as possible.

Note: Additional technical resources on smart clients are available from the Smart Client Developer Center at *http://msdn.microsoft.com/smartclient/*. The business value of smart clients is discussed on the Microsoft .NET site at *http://www.microsoft.com/net/smartclient/default.mspx*.

What Is a Smart Client?

To fully understand how smart clients combine the benefits of rich clients and thin clients, it is useful to examine the history and underlying principles behind the rich and thin client application models, and review some of the advantages and disadvantages associated with each.

Rich Client Applications

In the mid-1990s, the number of rich client applications developed for the Microsoft® Windows® operating system increased dramatically. These clients were designed to take advantage of the local hardware resources and the features of the client operating system platform.

Despite the impressive functionality of many of these applications, they have limitations. Many of these applications are stand-alone and operate on the client computer, with little or no awareness of the environment in which they operate. This environment includes the other computers and any services on the network, as well as any other applications on the user's computer. Very often, integration between applications is limited to using the cut or copy and paste features provided by Windows to transfer small amounts of data between applications.

There are technologies to help increase the connectivity of rich client applications. For example, two-tier applications allow multiple users to access common data residing on the network, and DCOM allows applications to become more distributed. (With DCOM, logic and state are no longer tied to the client computer, and instead are encapsulated within objects that are then distributed across multiple computers.) However, connected applications are considerably more complex to develop. As the size and complexity of these distributed applications grows, any tight coupling between client applications and the services they consume becomes increasingly difficult to maintain.

While rich clients typically provide a high-quality, responsive user experience and have good developer and platform support, they are very difficult to deploy and maintain. As the complexity of the applications and the client platform increases, so do the difficulties associated with deploying the application to the client computer in a reliable and secure way. One application can easily break another application if an incompatible shared component or library is deployed, a phenomenon known as *application fragility*. New versions of the application are typically made available by redeploying the entire application, which can increase an application fragility problem.

Thin Client Applications

The Internet provides an alternative to the traditional rich client model that solves many of the problems associated with application deployment and maintenance. Thin client, browser-based applications are deployed and updated on a central Web server; therefore, they remove the need to explicitly deploy and manage any part of the application to the client computer.

This model allows companies to very efficiently expose their applications to a large and diverse external audience. Because thin clients have proven to be effective at solving some of the deployment and manageability problems, they are now used to provide access to many line-of-business (LOB) applications to users within an organization, as well as access to externally facing applications to customers and partners. This is despite the fact that the needs and expectations of these two types of users are often radically different.

Thin client applications have some disadvantages. The browser must have a network connection at all times. This means that mobile users have no access to applications if they are disconnected, so they must reenter data when they return to the office. Also, common application features such as drag-and-drop, undo-redo, and context-sensitive help may be unavailable, which can reduce the usability of the application.

Because the vast majority of the application logic and state lives on the server, thin clients make frequent requests back to the server for data and processing. The browser must wait for a response before the user can continue to use the application; therefore, the application will typically be much less responsive than an equivalent rich client application. This problem is exacerbated in low bandwidth or high latency conditions, and the resulting performance problems can lead to a significant reduction in application usability and user efficiency. An LOB application that requires heavy data entry and/or frequent navigation across multiple windows can be particularly affected by this problem.

Smart Client Applications

Smart client applications can be designed to combine the benefits of a rich client application with the deployment and manageability strengths of a thin client application, although the precise nature of the balance between the two approaches depends on the exact scenario.

Smart client applications often have very diverse requirements, and so vary greatly in design and implementation. However, all smart clients share some or all of the following characteristics:

- Make use of local resources
- Make use of network resources
- Support occasionally connected users
- Provide intelligent installation and update
- Provide client device flexibility

Many applications do not need all of these characteristics. As you design your smart clients, you will need to carefully consider your application scenario and decide which of these characteristics your smart client application requires. Incorporating all of these characteristics into your application will require very careful planning and design, and in many cases you will need significant implementation resources.

Note: The .NET Framework helps you to implement many of the characteristics of smart client applications. Self-describing and tightly bound assemblies, along with support for isolated and side-by-side installation of multiple versions of an application, help to reduce application deployment and fragility problems associated with rich clients. The .NET Framework base class library provides extensive support for interaction with Web services, and provides Windows Forms. By using the common language runtime (CLR), you can use any .NET-supported language to develop your smart clients.

Using Local Resources

A well-designed smart client application takes maximum advantage of the fact that code and data are deployed on the client and executed and accessed locally. It provides an application with a rich and responsive user interface and powerful client-side processing capabilities. For example, it might enable the user to perform complex data manipulation, visualization, searching, or sorting operations.

Smart clients can take advantage of client-side hardware resources (such as telephones or barcode readers) and other software and applications. This makes them well suited to solve problems that a thin client application cannot solve well, such as point-of-sale applications. Smart clients can also take advantage of local software, such as Microsoft Office applications, or any installed LOB application on the client computer. Creating solutions that integrate with and coordinate multiple LOB applications allows your users to work more efficiently, make better decisions, and reduce data entry errors. Such solutions can also allow your application to be more tightly integrated with the user's working environment — for example by having a custom or familiar user interface — which can lead to decreased training costs.

Other client applications can be integrated or coordinated by the smart client application to provide a coherent and efficient overall solution. These applications should also be aware of the context in which the applications are being used, and should adapt to that context to aid the user as much as possible; for example, by preemptively caching appropriate and useful data according to the pattern of usage or the role of the user.

Maximizing the use of and integrating local resources into your smart client application enables your application to make better and more efficient use of the hardware that is already available to you. Very often, processing power, memory, and advanced graphical capabilities go unused. Using the resources on the client computer can also reduce server-side hardware requirements.

Using Network Resources

Smart clients can consume and use different services and data over the network. They are an effective way to retrieve data from many different sources and can be designed to analyze or aggregate the data, allowing the user to make more efficient and better informed decisions. For example, a smart client could use a mapping service to provide details on location and driving directions.

Smart client applications should be as connected as possible and should make use of the resources and services that are available to them over the network. They should not be stand-alone applications and should always form part of a larger distributed solution. At a minimum, a smart client application should use centralized services that help maintain the application and provide deployment and update services.

The connected nature of smart client applications allows them to provide valuable data aggregation, analysis, and transformation services. They can allow users to collaborate on tasks in real time or over a period of time. In many cases, a smart client application can provide portal-like capabilities to the user, allowing disparate data and services to be coordinated and integrated into an overall solution.

For details about how to design your smart clients to make use of connected services, see "Chapter 2, Getting Connected."

Supporting Occasionally Connected Users

Smart clients can be designed to provide functionality to users who are occasionally connected to the network, allowing the user to continue to work efficiently when explicitly offline, in low bandwidth or high latency network conditions, or when connectivity is intermittent. For mobile applications, smart clients can also optimize network bandwidth, for example by batching requests to the server to make better use of expensive connectivity.

Even when the client is connected to the network most of the time, smart client applications can improve performance and usability by caching data and managing the connection in an intelligent way. In a low bandwidth or high latency environment, for example, a smart client application can manage the connection in such a way that the usability and responsiveness of the application is not impaired and the user can continue to work efficiently.

Being able to work while disconnected or only occasionally connected increases user productivity and satisfaction. A smart client application should aim to provide as much functionality as possible when offline.

For details about how to design your smart client applications to support occasionally connected users, see Chapter 4, "Occasionally Connected Smart Clients."

Providing Intelligent Installation and Update

Some of the biggest problems with traditional rich clients occur when the application is deployed or updated. Many rich client applications have a large number of complex installation requirements and may share code by registering components and/or by installing DLLs in a common location, leading to application fragility and update difficulties.

Smart client applications can be designed to manage their deployment and update in a much more intelligent and flexible way than traditional rich client applications. They can avoid these common problems, which can help to reduce your application management costs.

There are a number of different ways to deploy smart clients. These include simply copying files onto a local computer, downloading code automatically from a central server using no-touch deployment, or deploying Windows Installer packages using an enterprise push technology such as Microsoft Systems Management Server (SMS). The method you choose will depend on your specific situation.

Smart client applications can update themselves automatically, either when they are run or in the background. This capability allows them to be updated on a role-by-role basis; updated in a staged manner, allowing applications to be rolled out to pilot groups or a limited set of users; or updated according to an established schedule.

The .NET Framework allows you to strongly name your application components, which means that the application can specify and run with the exact versions of the components with which it was built and tested. The .NET Framework allows applications to be isolated from each other so that installing one application will not break another application, and multiple versions of the same application can be deployed side by side. These features greatly simplify application deployment and remove many of the application fragility problems that were associated with rich client applications.

For more information about intelligent installation and updates, see Chapter 7, "Deployment."

Providing Client Device Flexibility

Smart clients can also provide a flexible and customizable client environment, allowing the user to configure the application to support his or her preferred way of working. Smart client applications are not restricted to desktop or laptop computers. As connectivity and the power of small-scale devices increases, the need for useful client applications that provide access to essential data and services on multiple devices also increases. Together with the .NET Compact Framework, the .NET Framework provides a common platform on which smart client applications can be built.

Smart clients can be designed to adapt to the host environment, providing appropriate functionality for the device on which they are running. For example, a smart client application designed to run on a Pocket PC should provide a user interface that is tuned to using a stylus on a small screen area.

In many cases, you will need to design multiple versions of a smart client application, each targeting a specific device type to take full advantage of the particular features supported by the device. Because small-scale devices are typically limited in their ability to deliver a full range of smart client application features, they may provide mobile access to only a subset of the data and services that a fully featured smart client application provides, or they may be used to collect and aggregate data when the user is mobile. This data can then be analyzed or processed by a more fully featured smart client application or by a server-side application.

An awareness of the capabilities and usage environment of the target device, whether it is a desktop, laptop, tablet, or mobile device, and the ability to tailor the application to provide the most appropriate functionality are essential features of many smart client applications.

Note: This guide does not cover architectural and design details specific to the development of smart client applications to be run on mobile devices, but many of the topics that are covered are equally relevant whether the application is run on a desktop computer or another device.

Types of Smart Clients

Smart clients vary greatly in design and implementation, both in application requirements and in the number of scenarios and environments in which they can be used. Smart clients therefore can take many different forms and styles. These forms can be divided into three broad categories according to the platform that the smart client application is targeting:

- Windows smart client applications
- Office smart client applications
- Mobile smart client applications

It is common for a smart client application to target one or more of these platforms, depending on the role of the user and the functionality required. Such flexibility is one of the key strengths of smart client applications.

The remainder of this guide concentrates on issues that are common to all three types of smart client applications, rather than providing a detailed explanation of issues that affect each individual category. However, it is useful to briefly examine each type in turn so that you can determine which style of application might be best for your situation.

Windows Smart Client Applications

When you think of a rich client application, you may typically think of a desktop application that uses available system resources and that provides a rich user interface. Windows-targeted smart client applications represent an evolution of traditional rich client applications, and provide specific and targeted functionality.

These kinds of applications typically use Windows Forms to provide a familiar Windows-style user interface, where the application itself provides much of the functionality and does not rely on another application to provide the main user interface. Such smart clients can range from simple applications deployed over HTTP to very sophisticated applications.

A Windows smart client application is suitable in situations where an application needs to be deployed and accessed as a familiar desktop-type application. These types of applications typically provide the majority of their functionality themselves but can integrate with or coordinate other applications when appropriate. They provide application functionality tuned to particular tasks to provide specific or high-performance processing or graphical capabilities.

Windows smart client applications are typically most suitable for applications that run on desktop, laptop, or tablet PCs. In addition, they generally provide functionality that is not tightly associated with a particular document or document type.

These kinds of Windows smart client applications can be used in a wide variety of situations, for instance as LOB, financial, scientific, or collaborative applications. Examples of these kinds of applications are Microsoft Money and the Microsoft Outlook® messaging and collaboration client.

Office Smart Client Applications

Microsoft Office System 2003 provides you with a useful platform on which to build smart client applications, especially in an enterprise setting. With an Office smart client solution, you can integrate data sources, accessed through Web services, with the features of Word 2003, Excel 2003, InfoPath 2003, or other Office applications to develop smart client solutions.

Such Office smart client applications can become an integrated part of an organization's information management cycle, not just static containers for document data. They can provide context-sensitive data as the user works within a document, as well as workflow and task guidance, data analysis, collaboration, reporting, and presentation features that turn data exposed by Web services into useful information.

Microsoft Office supports XML and separates the data from other aspects of a document so that it can be reused by other applications. Because application data in Microsoft Office can be described by the same customer-defined XML schema across multiple applications, developers can integrate that data into smart client applications.

Microsoft Office 2003 has a number of key features and options for building smart client solutions. These include:

- **Smart tags**. Smart tags give applications a way to provide users with context-sensitive data pertaining to the contents of a document and allow them to easily see and use relevant information when working within a document. For example, smart tags can be used to provide account status for customers as those customers are referenced within a document, or they can be used to provide order status information as an order ID is typed. This contextualized feedback permits users to make more informed decisions as they work.

- **Smart documents**. Smart documents provide a more powerful way for the user to interact with documents and business Web services. Smart documents are a new type of solution model for Word 2003 and Excel 2003 that have an underlying XML structure and a customized task pane. The task pane can be used to display contextual information, tasks, tools, next steps, and other relevant information to the user. The user is able to initiate other actions and tasks by interacting with the task pane, allowing comprehensive business solutions to be constructed.

- **Microsoft Visual Studio® Tools for the Microsoft Office System**. This suite of tools enables developers to create managed code Office smart client applications by using the Microsoft Visual Studio .NET 2003 development system. Developers can separate document solutions from the underlying code (an alternative to previous smart client models that contained Visual Basic for Applications macros with custom logic). Using managed code with Microsoft Office provides developers with more effective options for creating, deploying, and managing updates for smart client solutions.

- **Microsoft Office InfoPath™ 2003**. InfoPath 2003 is an application that can gather structured data from the user by using a form-like interface. InfoPath 2003 provides support for XML Web services, a form-based user interface, and support for standard technologies such as WSDL and UDDI. InfoPath 2003 supports limited offline use by allowing the user to interact with the form when offline and then allowing the user to forward the form to a Web service when the user is online.

This guide does not attempt to cover any of the issues specific to Office smart clients, but most of the topics that are covered are entirely relevant to the smart client applications discussed above.

Mobile Smart Client Applications

Mobile smart clients are applications that run on smart devices — Pocket PCs, Smartphones, and other small form factor devices such as set-top boxes. These applications are developed using the .NET Compact Framework, which is a subset of the full .NET Framework.

The .NET Compact Framework has many of the features of the full .NET Framework, supports XML, and consumes Web services. It is optimized for use on small form factor devices, and it includes the Windows Forms designer for developing the user interface.

By using the Visual Studio .NET Smart Device Projects, you can develop smart clients that will run on the .NET Compact Framework. This approach allows you to develop, test, and debug an application by using Visual Studio .NET on an emulator of the small form factor device. The use of an emulator significantly speeds up development and testing of these types of applications.

Mobile smart client applications are typically used to provide mobile access to essential data and services, or to collect and aggregate data when the user is mobile. Examples of these types of applications are insurance and financial data-gathering applications, inventory management applications, and personal productivity management applications.

This guide does not specifically focus on mobile smart client applications, although many of the architectural issues and solutions that it discusses are relevant to smart devices.

Choosing Between Smart Clients and Thin Clients

To choose the right application architecture for your situation, you must consider a number of factors. To determine whether a smart client approach is the most suitable for your application, carefully consider your current and future business application needs. If your application is based on an unsuitable architecture, it may fail to meet the requirements and expectations of the users and the business as a whole. Changing the architecture later to meet new requirements or to take advantage of new opportunities may be extremely expensive.

A thin client architecture is often the most appropriate if you need to make an externally facing application available to a diverse external audience, while a smart client architecture is often the most suitable for an internal application that needs to integrate with or coordinate other client-side applications or hardware, or that is required to work offline or provide specific high-performance functionality through a responsive user interface.

In reality these two approaches overlap to a great extent, and each has distinct advantages and disadvantages. You will only be able to choose the right approach after you carefully consider your requirements and understand how each approach would apply in your situation. Use Table 1.1 to help you choose between a smart client and thin client architecture.

Table 1.1: Features of Thin Clients and Smart Clients

Feature	Thin client	Smart client
Provides a rich user interface	Yes, but difficult to develop, test, and debug. Generally ties the application to a single browser.	Yes. Easier to develop, test, and debug.
Can take advantage of hardware resources on local computer	Yes, but only through COM components.	Yes
Can interact with other local applications	No	Yes
Can be multithreaded	No	Yes
Can function offline	No	Yes
Can perform well in low bandwidth and high latency environments	No	Yes
Easy to deploy	Yes	Varies. Difficulty depends on application requirements.
Low maintenance and change management costs	Yes	Varies. Costs depend on application requirements.
Can be deployed to a wide variety of clients with varying capabilities	Yes, although more complex thin clients may require a single browser.	Yes. Can be deployed on any platform that supports the .NET Framework (including the .NET Compact Framework).

Smart Client Architectural Challenges

The architectural challenges of smart clients differ from those of thin clients, and you will need to account for them in your application design. The benefits of smart client applications are significant, but you can realize them only if you address these challenges appropriately.

Smart clients allow data and logic to be distributed to the client computer, whereas thin clients tend to keep the data and logic centralized on the Web server and other back-end services. Although the smart client approach allows you to make the application more efficient, with no round trips to the server to determine next steps, you need to consider that the application and its data are now more widely distributed than with thin client applications, and modify your design accordingly.

If you are implementing business rules on the client, you will need to update those rules as required, without updating the entire application. This may mean that you use differing mechanisms for updating the application and updating business rules within the application.

By caching data on the client, you can significantly improve the performance and usability of an application, but you must ensure that the data is refreshed appropriately and that stale data is not used. Because many users can access and use the same data, you must also consider the effects of data concurrency. Your application must be able to handle data conflicts or reconciliation issues that arise because the application is now more widely distributed and can operate while offline. Chapter 3, "Handling Data," covers these issues in depth.

The .NET Framework provides a great deal of flexibility in how your smart client applications can be hosted. Applications can be run as traditional desktop applications or can be hosted within Office or Microsoft Internet Explorer. Many combinations are possible. For instance, a Windows Forms application can host Internet Explorer or Office components, and any host can subsume any other.

You can factor volatile application logic (for example, business rules governing volume order discounts) into assemblies that are downloaded on demand over HTTP. Doing so obviates the need to deploy new versions of the client application as new application logic is developed. You can use the same model for additional (or infrequently used) application features, so that initial application size is kept to a minimum, and additional features are installed on an as-needed basis.

You may choose to deploy your smart clients as composite applications, where many applications combine to form a coherent solution. Such solutions can be formed by coupling desktop applications, or by providing a generic shell application that houses multiple lightweight applications that together form the solution.

Composite applications are particularly useful in situations where users have to access many applications to do their work. For example, customer service agents in call centers typically have to work with many LOB applications, including desktop, browser-based, and terminal-based applications. All such LOB applications can be hosted within a generic Windows Forms application that provides integration between them, greatly simplifying the user's job and, most importantly, reducing the time spent on a particular call. By providing a generic shell to host these LOB applications, common infrastructure features, such as security, deployment, window management, application integration, auditing, and so on, can be developed, tested, and reused across different solutions, freeing the developers of the LOB applications to focus on business functionality.

The advent of service-oriented architectures means that you can design smart clients to make use of network services. All such services are provided in an industry-standard way, which improves interoperability, developer tool support, and the ease with which new features can be built into the smart client application.

Scope of This Guide

This guide is focused on the architectural and design issues surrounding smart client applications built on the Microsoft .NET technologies. It assumes that you are building your smart client applications using the Microsoft .NET Framework and are using Microsoft .NET Windows Forms to build any user interface.

The guide does not cover implementation issues in depth. In particular, the details of implementing a smart client application on Microsoft Office 2003 or on a mobile device are not covered, although many of the issues covered in this guide are relevant to smart client applications — whether they are stand-alone Windows Forms, Office, or mobile device applications.

How to Use This Guide

This guide is designed to be used in one of two ways. First, the guide is structured to provide a fairly comprehensive overview of the architectural and design issues you might face when building a smart client application. Reading the guide from start to finish will give you the fullest understanding of the issues you might face and how to overcome them.

Alternatively, if you prefer to delve into the issues surrounding a specific topic, you can read chapters individually for self-contained discussions of the relevant issues.

Who Should Read This Guide

This guide is intended for software architects and developers who are developing smart client applications built on Microsoft .NET technologies.

Prerequisites

To benefit fully from this guide, you should have an understanding of the following technologies and concepts:

- The Microsoft .NET Framework
- Microsoft Visual Studio .NET 2003 development tool
- Microsoft® Visual C#® development tool
- Extensible Markup Language (XML)
- Message Queuing (MSMQ)
- Multithreading
- Relational database operation
- Distributed application design and architecture

Note: For more information about distributed application design and architecture, see *http://msdn.microsoft.com/library/default.asp?url=/library/en-us/vsent7 /html/vxoriDesignConsiderationsForDistributedApplications.asp* and *http://msdn.microsoft.com/library/default.asp?url=/library/en-us/vsent7 /html/vxoriplanningdistributedapplications.asp*.

Chapter Outlines

This guide consists of the following chapters, each of which deals with a specific issue relevant to smart clients. Each chapter is designed to be read, in whole or in part, according to your needs.

Chapter 1: Introduction

This chapter gives a high-level description of smart client applications and describes some of their basic properties and benefits. It then discusses some of the high-level architectural issues and provides guidance to help you determine if a smart client architecture is right for your application.

Chapter 2: Handling Data

In smart clients, application data is available on the client. This data needs to be managed appropriately to make sure that it is kept valid, consistent, and secure. If the data is provided by a server application, the smart client application may cache the data to improve performance or to enable offline usage. If your smart client application provides the ability to modify data locally, the client changes have to be synchronized with the server-side application at a later time. This chapter examines the various considerations for handling data on the client, including data caching, data concurrency, and the use of datasets and Windows Forms data binding.

Chapter 3: Getting Connected

Smart client applications often form one part of a larger distributed application, so they are frequently connected to a network and interact with network resources such as Web services, along with components or processes on the client computer itself. This chapter describes a number of ways in which your application can connect to and use these resources, and discusses the strengths and weaknesses of each.

Chapter 4: Occasionally Connected Smart Clients

This chapter contains a discussion of the issues you might face when designing and building smart client applications that are occasionally connected to the network. The chapter covers the concept of connectivity, describes the two main approaches to implementing offline capabilities, and discusses some of the things you need to consider to make your application available when offline.

Chapter 5: Security Considerations

This chapter covers the issues of smart client security. Smart clients distribute logic and data to the client computer; therefore, the security concerns are different from those associated with thin a client application, where data and logic are confined more to the server. This chapter discusses data security, authentication, authorization, and the role of code access security within a smart client application.

Chapter 6: Using Multiple Threads

This chapter discusses the issues surrounding the use of multiple threads in a smart client application. To maximize the responsiveness of your smart client applications, you need to carefully consider how and when to use multiple threads. Threads can significantly improve the usability and performance of your application, but they require very careful consideration when you determine how they will interact with the user interface.

Chapter 7: Deploying and Updating Smart Client Applications

Smart clients do not suffer from the deployment and update problems traditionally associated with rich client applications. Features provided by the .NET Framework and the Windows platform help you to avoid many problems associated with traditional rich client deployment. This chapter describes how to best use these features and how to choose between the deployment and update mechanisms available.

Chapter 8: Smart Client Application Performance

This chapter examines techniques that you can use as you architect and design your smart client applications to ensure that you optimize their performance. It looks at a number of tools and techniques you can use to identify performance problems in your smart client applications.

Summary

Thin clients and smart clients can each be used to provide LOB applications to your organization. However, each type of client has its advantages and disadvantages. When designing your application, you will need to carefully consider the specifics of your situation before you can determine which is more appropriate. This chapter has explained how smart clients evolved and the features that are associated with them. You can now use the rest of this guide to help you determine how to design and implement smart clients in your own organization.

More Information

The following resources provide more information about *patterns & practices*, smart clients, and other application blocks that you can use to find specific guidance.

- *patterns & practices* Web site at *http://www.microsoft.com/resources/practices /default.mspx*
- Patterns and Practices Library at *http://www.microsoft.com/resources/practices /completelist.asp*
- Overview of Smart Client Applications in the Microsoft Office System on MSDN® at *http://msdn.microsoft.com/library/default.asp?url=/library/en-us/odc_ip2003_ta/html /odc_IPOffice2003SmartClient.asp*
- Application Architecture for .NET: Designing Applications and Services on MSDN at *http://msdn.microsoft.com/library/default.asp?url=/library/en-us/dnbda/html /distapp.asp*

2

Handling Data

In smart clients, application data is available on the client. If your smart clients are to function effectively, it is essential that this data be managed appropriately to make sure that it is kept valid, consistent, and secure.

Application data can be made available to the client by a server-side application (for example, through a Web service), or the application can use its own local data. If the data is provided by a server application, the smart client application may cache the data to improve performance or to enable offline usage. In this case, you need to decide how the client application should handle data that is out of date with respect to the server.

If your smart client application provides the ability to modify data locally, the client changes have to be synchronized with the server-side application at a later time. In this case, you have to decide how the client application can handle data conflicts and how to keep track of the changes that need to be sent to the server.

You need to carefully consider these and a number of other issues when designing your smart client application. This chapter examines the various considerations for handling data on the client, including:

- Types of data
- Caching data
- Data concurrency
- Using ADO.NET datasets to manage data
- Windows Forms data binding

A number of other issues related to handling data are not discussed in this chapter. In particular, data handling security issues are discussed in Chapter 5, "Security Considerations," and offline considerations are discussed in Chapter 4, "Occasionally Connected Smart Clients."

Types of Data

Smart clients generally have to handle two categories of data:

- Read-only reference data
- Transient data

Typically, these types of data need to be handled in different ways, so it is useful to examine each of them in more detail.

Read-Only Reference Data

Read-only reference data is data that is not changed by the client and that is used by the client for reference purposes. Therefore, from the client's point of view, the data is read-only data, and the client performs no update, insert, or delete operations on it. Read-only reference data is readily cached on the client. Reference data has a number of uses in a smart client application, including:

- **Providing static reference or lookup data**. Examples include product information, price lists, shipping options, and prices.
- **Supporting data validation, allowing data entered by the user to be checked for correctness**. An example is checking entered dates against a delivery schedule.
- **Helping to communicate with remote services**. An example is converting a user selection to a product ID locally and then sending the information to a Web service.
- **Presenting data**. Examples include presenting Help text or user interface labels.

By storing and using reference data on the client, you can reduce the amount of data that needs to travel from client to server, improve the performance of your application, help enable offline capabilities, and provide early data validation, which increases the usability of your application.

Although read-only reference data cannot be changed by the client, it can be changed on the server (for example, by an administrator or supervisor). You need to determine a strategy for updating the client when changes to the data occur. Such a strategy could involve pushing changes out to the client when a change occurs or pulling changes from the server at certain time intervals or prior to certain actions on the client. However, because the data is read-only at the client, you do not need to keep track of client-side changes. This simplifies the way in which read-only reference data needs to be handled.

Transient Data

Transient data can be changed on the client as well as the server. Generally, transient data changes as a direct or indirect result of user input and manipulation. In this case, changes that are made on either the client or server need to be synchronized at some point. This type of data has a number of uses in a smart client, including:

- **Adding new information**. Examples include adding banking transactions or customer details.
- **Modifying existing information**. An example is updating customer details.
- **Deleting existing information**. An example is removing a customer from a database.

One of the most challenging aspects of dealing with transient data on smart clients is that it can generally be modified on multiple clients at the same time. This problem is exacerbated when the data is very volatile, because changes are more likely to conflict with one another.

You need to keep track of any client-side changes that you make to transient data. Until the data is synchronized with the server and any conflicts have been resolved, you should not consider transient data to be confirmed. You should be very careful not to rely on unconfirmed data to make important decisions or use it as the basis for other local changes without carefully considering how data consistency can be guaranteed even in the event of a synchronization failure.

For more details about the issues surrounding handling data when offline and how to handle data synchronization, see Chapter 4, "Occasionally Connected Smart Clients."

Caching Data

Smart clients often need to cache data locally, whether it is read-only reference data or transient data. Caching data has the potential to improve performance in your application and provide the data necessary to work offline. However, you need to carefully consider which data is cached on the client, how that data is to be managed, and the context in which that data can be used.

To enable data caching, your smart client application should implement some form of caching infrastructure that can handle the data caching details transparently. Your caching infrastructure should include one or both of the following caching mechanisms:

- **Short-term data caching**. Caching data in memory is good for performance but is not persistent, so you may need to pull data from the source when the application is re-run. Doing so may prevent your application from operating when offline.

- **Long-term data caching**. Caching data in a persistent medium, such as isolated storage or the local file system, allows you to use the application when there is no connectivity to the server. You may choose to combine long-term storage with short-term storage to improve performance.

Regardless of the caching mechanisms you adopt, you should ensure that only data to which the user has access is made available to the client. Also, sensitive data cached on the client requires careful handling to ensure that it is kept secure. Therefore, you may need to encrypt the data as it is transferred to the client and as it is stored on the client. For more information, see "Handling Sensitive Data" in Chapter 5, "Security Considerations."

As you design your smart client to support data caching, you should consider providing a mechanism for your client to request fresh data, regardless of the state of the cache. This means that you can be sure that the application is ready to perform new transactions without using stale data. You may also configure your client to pre-fetch data so that it can mitigate the risk of being offline when cached data expires.

Wherever possible, you should associate some form of metadata with the data to enable the client to manage the data in an intelligent way. Such metadata can be used to specify the data's identity and any constraints or desired behaviors associated with the data. Your client-side caching infrastructure should consume this metadata and use it to handle the cached data appropriately.

All data that is cached on the client should be uniquely identifiable (for example, through a version number or date stamp), so that it can be properly identified when determining whether it needs to be updated. Your caching infrastructure is then able to ask the server whether the data that it has is currently valid and determine if any updates are required.

Metadata can also be used to specify constraints or behaviors that relate to the usage and handling of the cached data. Examples include:

- **Temporal constraints**. These constraints specify the time or date range in which the cached data can be used. When the data becomes stale or expires, it can be dropped from the cache or automatically refreshed by obtaining the latest data from the server. In some cases, it may be appropriate to let the client use out-of-date reference data and map it to up-to-date data when it is synchronized with the server.
- **Geographic constraints**. Some data may be appropriate only for a particular region. For example, you may have different price lists for different locations. Your caching infrastructure can be used to access and store data on a per-location basis.
- **Security requirements**. Data that is specifically intended for a particular user can be encrypted to ensure that only the appropriate user can access it. In this case, the data is provided already encrypted, and the user has to provide the credentials to the caching infrastructure to allow the data to be decrypted.

- **Business rules**. You may have business rules associated with your cached data that dictate how it should be used. For example, your caching infrastructure may take into consideration the role of the user to determine what data is provided to him or her and how it is handled.

The metadata associated with the data enables your caching infrastructure to handle the data appropriately so that your application does not have to be concerned with data caching issues or implementation details. You can pass the metadata associated with the reference data within the data itself, or you can use an out-of-band mechanism. The exact mechanism used to transport the metadata to the client depends on how your application communicates with the network services. When using Web services, using SOAP headers to communicate the metadata to the client is a good solution.

The differences between read-only reference data and transient data sometimes mean that you need to use two caches, one for reference data and one for transient data. Reference data is read-only on the client and does not need to be synchronized back with the server, but it does need to be refreshed occasionally to reflect any changes and updates made on the server.

Transient data can be changed on the client as well as the server. With data in the cache being updated sometimes on the client, sometimes on the server, and sometimes on both, any changes made to the data on the client need to be synchronized with the server at some point. If the data has changed on the server in the meantime, a data conflict occurs and needs to be handled appropriately.

To help ensure that data consistency is maintained, and to avoid using data inappropriately, you should be careful to keep track of any changes that you make to transient data on the client. Such changes are *uncommitted* or *tentative* until they are successfully synchronized or confirmed with the server.

You should design your smart client application so that it can differentiate between data that has been successfully synchronized with the server and data that is still tentative. This distinction helps your application detect and handle data conflicts more easily. Also, you may want to restrict the application or the user from making important decisions or initiating important actions based on tentative data. Such data should not be relied on until it has been synchronized with the server. By using an appropriate caching infrastructure, you can keep track of tentative and confirmed data.

The Caching Application Block

The Caching Application Block is a Microsoft® .NET Framework extension that allows developers to easily cache data from service providers. It was built and designed to encapsulate Microsoft's recommended practices for caching in .NET Framework applications as described in *Caching Architecture Guide for .NET Framework Applications* at *http://msdn.microsoft.com/library/default.asp?url=/library/en-us/dnbda/html /CachingArch.asp*.

The overall architecture of the caching block is shown in Figure 2.1.

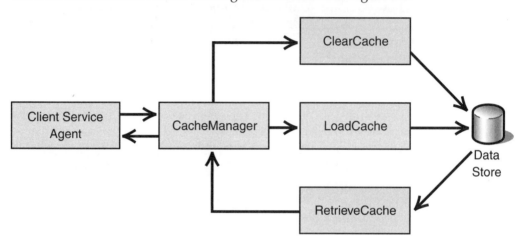

Figure 2.1
Caching block workflow

The caching workflow consists of the following steps:

1. A client or service agent makes a request to the **CacheManager** for cached data items.

2. If the item is already cached, the **CacheManager** retrieves the item from storage and returns it as a **CacheItem** object. If the item is not already cached, the client is notified.

3. After retrieving noncached data from a service provider, the client sends the data to the **CacheManager**. The **CacheManager** adds a signature (that is, metadata), such as a key, expiration, or priority, to the item and loads it into the cache.

4. The **CacheService** monitors the lifetime of **CacheItems**. When a **CacheItem** expires, the **CacheService** removes it and, optionally, calls a callback delegate.

5. The **CacheService** can also flush all items from the cache.

The caching block offers a variety of caching expiration options, which are described in Table 2.1.

Table 2.1: Caching Block Expiration Options

Class	Description
AbsoluteTime	Use to set the absolute time for an expiration.
ExtendedFormatTime	Use to set an expiration based on an expression (such as every minute or every Monday).
FileDependency	Use to set an expiration based on whether a file is changed.
SlidingTime	Use to set the lifetime for an item by specifying an expiration based on when an item is last accessed.

The following storage mechanisms are available for the caching block:

● **Memory-mapped file (MMF)**. MMFs are best suited for a client-based, high-performance caching scenario. You can use MMFs to develop a cache that can be shared across multiple application domains and processes within the same computer. The .NET Framework does not support MMFs, so any implementation of an MMF cache runs as unmanaged code and does not benefit from any .NET Framework features, including memory management features (such as garbage collection) and security features (such as code access security).

● **Singleton object**. A .NET remoting singleton object can be used to cache data that can be shared across processes in one or several computers. This is done by implementing a caching service using a singleton object that serves multiple clients through .NET remoting. Singleton caching is simple to implement, but it lacks the performance and scalability provided by solutions based on Microsoft SQL Server™.

● **Microsoft SQL Server 2000 database**. SQL Server 2000 storage is best suited to an application that requires high durability or when you need to cache a very large amount of data. Because the cache service needs to access SQL Server over a network and the data is retrieved using database queries, data access is relatively slow.

● **Microsoft SQL Server Desktop Engine (MSDE)**. MSDE is a lightweight database alternative to SQL Server 2000. It provides reliability and security features but has a smaller client footprint than SQL Server, so it requires less setup and configuration. Because MSDE supports SQL, developers also gain much of the power of a database. You can migrate an MSDE database to a SQL Server database if necessary.

Data Concurrency

As mentioned earlier, one problem with using smart clients is that changes to the data held on the server can occur before any client-side changes are synchronized with the server. You need a mechanism to ensure that when the data is synchronized, any data conflicts are handled appropriately and the resultant data is consistent and correct. The ability for data to be updated by more than one client is known as data concurrency.

There are two approaches that you could use to handle data concurrency:

- **Pessimistic concurrency**. Pessimistic concurrency allows one client to maintain a lock over the data to prevent any other clients from modifying the data until the client's own changes are complete. In such cases, if another client attempts to modify the data, the attempt fails or is blocked until the lock's owner releases the lock.

  Pessimistic concurrency can be problematic, because a single user or client may hold on to a lock for a significant period of time, possibly inadvertently. Therefore, the lock could prevent important resources, such as database rows or files, from being released in a timely manner, which can seriously affect the scalability and usability of the application. However, pessimistic concurrency may be appropriate when you need to have complete control over changes made to important resources. Note that it cannot be used if your clients are to work offline, because they are not able to put a lock on data.

- **Optimistic concurrency**. Optimistic concurrency does not lock the data .To decide whether an update is actually required, the original data can be sent along with the update request and the changed data. The original data is then checked against the current data to see if it has been updated in the meantime. If the original data and the current data match, the update is executed; otherwise, the request is denied, producing an optimistic failure. To optimize this process, you can use a time stamp or an update counter in the data instead of sending the original data, and in this case only the time stamp or counter needs to be checked.

  Optimistic concurrency provides a good mechanism for updating master data that does not change very often, such as a customer's phone number or address. Optimistic concurrency allows everyone to read the data, and in situations where updates are less likely than read operations, the risk of an optimistic failure may be acceptable. Optimistic concurrency may not be suitable in situations where the data is changed often and where the optimistic updates are likely to fail often.

In most smart client scenarios, including those in which clients are to work offline, optimistic concurrency is the correct approach because it allows multiple clients to work on data at the same time without unnecessarily locking data and affecting all other clients.

For more information about optimistic and pessimistic concurrency, see "Optimistic Concurrency" in the *.NET Framework Developer's Guide* at *http://msdn.microsoft.com/library/default.asp?url=/library/en-us/cpguide/html /cpconoptimisticconcurrency.asp*.

Using ADO.NET DataSets to Manage Data

A **DataSet** is an object that represents one or more relational database tables. Datasets store data in a disconnected cache. The structure of a dataset is similar to that of a relational database: It exposes a hierarchical object model of tables, rows, and columns. In addition, it contains constraints and relationships defined for the dataset.

An ADO.NET **DataSet** contains a collection of zero or more tables represented by **DataTable** objects. A **DataTable** is defined in the **System.Data** namespace and represents a single table of memory-resident data. It contains a collection of columns represented by a **DataColumnCollection** and constraints represented by a **ConstraintCollection**, which together define the schema of the table. A **DataTable** also contains a collection of rows represented by the **DataRowCollection**, which contains the data in the table. Along with its current state, a **DataRow** retains both its current and original versions to identify changes to the values stored in the row.

Datasets can be strongly typed or untyped. A typed **DataSet** inherits from the **DataSet** base class but adds strong typed language functionality to the **DataSet**, allowing users to access content in a more strongly typed programmatic manner. Either type can be used when building applications. However, the Microsoft Visual Studio® development system has more support for typed datasets, and they make programming with the dataset easier and less error prone.

Datasets are particularly useful in a smart client environment, because they offer functionality that helps clients to work with data while offline. They can keep track of local changes made to the data, which helps to synchronize the data with the server and reconcile data conflicts, and they can be used to merge data from different sources.

For more information about working with datasets, see "Introduction to Datasets" in *Visual Basic and Visual C# Concepts* at *http://msdn.microsoft.com/library/default.asp?url= /library/en-us/vbcon/html/vbconDataSets.asp*.

Merging Data with Datasets

Datasets have the ability to merge the contents of **DataSet**, **DataTable**, or **DataRow** objects into existing datasets. This functionality is particularly useful for keeping track of changes on the client and merging with updated content from the server. Figure 2.2 shows a smart client requesting an update from the Web service, and the new data being returned as a data transfer object (DTO). A DTO is an enterprise pattern that allows you to package all the data required to communicate with a Web service into one object. Using a DTO often means that you can make a single call to a Web service rather than multiple calls.

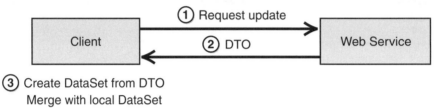

③ Create DataSet from DTO
   Merge with local DataSet

Figure 2.2
Merging data on the client by using datasets

In this example, when the DTO is returned to the client, the DTO is used to create a new dataset locally on the client.

Note: After a merge operation, ADO.NET does not automatically change the row state from modified to unchanged. Therefore, after merging the new dataset with the local client dataset, you need to invoke the **AccceptChanges** method on your dataset to reset the **RowState** property to unchanged.

For more information about using datasets, see "Merging DataSet Contents" in the *.NET Framework Developer's Guide* at *http://msdn.microsoft.com/library/default.asp?url= /library/en-us/cpguide/html/cpconmergingdatasetcontents.asp*.

Increasing the Performance of Datasets

Datasets can often contain a large amount of data, which, if passed over the network, can lead to performance problems. Fortunately, with ADO.NET **DataSets**, you can use the **GetChanges** method on your datasets to ensure that only the data that is changed in a dataset is communicated between the client and the server, packaging the data in a DTO. Then the data is merged into the dataset at its destination.

Figure 2.3 shows a smart client that makes changes to local data and uses the **GetChanges** method on a dataset to submit only changed data to the server. The data is transferred to a DTO for performance reasons.

Figure 2.3
Using a DTO to improve performance

The **GetChanges** method can be used for smart client applications that need to go offline. When an application is again online, you can use the **GetChanges** method to determine what information has changed and then generate a DTO to communicate with the Web service to ensure that the changes are submitted to a database.

Windows Forms Data Binding

Windows Forms data binding enables you to connect the user interface of your application to the application's underlying data. Windows Forms data binding supports bidirectional binding so you can bind a data structure to the user interface, display the current data values to the user, allow the user to edit the data, and then update the underlying data automatically, using the values entered by the user.

You can use Windows Forms data binding to bind virtually any data structure or object to any property of the user interface controls. You can bind a single item of data to a single property of a control, or you can bind more complex data (for example, a collection of data items or a database table) to the control so it can display all of the data in a data grid or list box.

Note: You can bind any object that supports one or more public properties. You can bind only to public properties of your classes and not to public members.

Windows Forms data binding allows you to provide a flexible, data-driven user interface with your applications. You can use data binding to provide customizable control over the look and feel of your user interface (for example, by binding to control properties such as the background or foreground color, size, image, or icon).

Data binding has many uses. For example, it can be used to:

- Display read-only data to users.
- Allow users to update data from the user interface.
- Provide master-detail views on data.
- Allow users to explore complex related data items.
- Provide lookup table functionality, allowing the user interface to connect user-friendly display names.

This section examines some features of data binding and discusses some of the data binding features that you frequently need to implement in a smart client application.

For in-depth information about data binding, see "Windows Forms Data Binding and Objects" at *http://msdn.microsoft.com/library/default.asp?url=/library/en-us/dnadvnet/html /vbnet02252003.asp*.

Windows Forms Data Binding Architecture

Windows Forms data binding provides a flexible infrastructure to bidirectionally connect data to the user the interface. Figure 2.4 shows a schematic representation of the overall architecture of Windows Forms data binding.

Windows Form

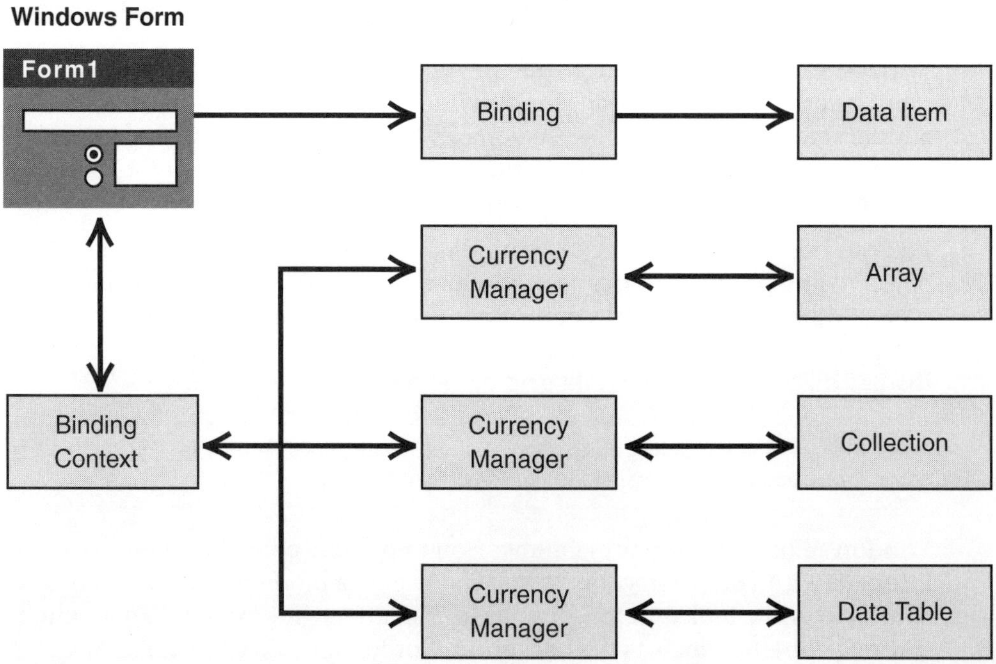

Figure 2.4
Architecture of Windows Forms data binding

Windows Forms data binding uses the following objects:

- **Data source**. Data sources are the objects that contain the data to be bound to the user interface. Data providers can be any object that has public properties, an array or a collection that supports the IList interface or an instance of a complex data class (for example, **DataSet** or **DataTable**).

- **CurrencyManager**. The **CurrencyManager** object keeps track of the current position of the data within an array, collection, or table that is bound to the user interface. The **CurrencyManager** allows you to bind a collection of data to the user interface and to navigate through that data, updating the user interface to reflect the currently selected item within the collection.

- **PropertyManager**. The **PropertyManager** object is responsible for maintaining the current property of an object that is bound to a control. Both the **PropertyManager** and **CurrencyManager** classes inherit from a common base class, **BindingManagerBase**. All data providers bound to a control to have an associated **CurrencyManager** or **PropertyManager** object.

- **BindingContext**. Each Windows Form has a default **BindingContext** object that keeps track of all of the **CurrencyManager** and **PropertyManager** objects on the form. The **BindingContext** object allows you to easily retrieve the **CurrencyManager** or **PropertyManager** object for a specific data source. You can assign a specific **BindingContext** object to a container control (such as a **GroupBox**, **Panel**, or **TabControl**) that contains data-bound controls. Doing so allows each part of your form to be managed by its own **CurrencyManager** or **PropertyManager** objects.

- **Binding**. The **Binding** objects are used to create and maintain a simple binding between a single property of a control and either the property of another object or the property of the current object in a list of objects.

Binding Data to Windows Forms Controls

There are a number of properties and methods that you can use to bind to specific Windows Forms controls. Table 2.2 shows some of the more important ones.

Table 2.2: Properties and Methods for Binding to Windows Forms Controls

Property or method	Windows Forms control	Description
DataSource property	ListControls (for example, ListBox or Combo Box), DataGrid control	Allows you to specify the data provider object to be bound to the user interface control.
DisplayMember property	ListControls	Allows you to specify the member of the data provider to be displayed to the user.
ValueMember property	ListControls	Allows you to specify the value associated with the displayed value for the internal use of your application.
DataMember property	DataGrid control	If the data source contains more than one source of data (for example, if you specify a **DataSet** that contains multiple tables), use the **DataMember** property to specify the one to be bound to the grid. (See note following table.)
SetDataBinding method	DataGrid control	Allows you to reset the **DataSource** method at run time.

Note: If the **DataSource** is a **DataTable**, **DataView**, collection, or array, setting the **DataMember** property is not required.

You can also use the **DataBindings** collection property available on all Windows Forms control objects to add **Binding** objects explicitly to any control object. **Binding** objects are used to bind a single property on the control to a single data member of the data provider. The following code example adds a binding between the **Text** property of a text box control to the customer name in the customers table of a data set.

```
textBox1.DataBindings.Add(
        new Binding( "Text", dataset, "customers.customerName" ) );
```

When you construct a **Binding** instance with the **Binding** constructor, you must specify the name of the control property to bind to, the data source, and the navigation path that resolves to a list or property in the data source. The navigation path can be an empty string, a single property name, or a period-delimited hierarchy of names. You can use a hierarchical navigation path to navigate through data tables and relations in a **DataSet** object, or over an object model where an object's properties return instances to other objects. If you set the navigation path to an empty string, the **ToString** method is called on the underlying data source object.

Note: If a property is read-only (that is, the object does not support a set operation for that property), data binding does not by default make the bound Windows Forms control read-only. This can lead to confusion for the user, because the user can edit the value in the user interface, but the value in the bound object will not be updated. Therefore, make sure the read-only flags are set to **true** for all Windows Forms controls that are bound to read-only properties.

Binding Controls to DataSets

It is often useful to bind controls to datasets. Doing so allows you to display the dataset data in a data grid, and it allows the user to easily update the data. You can bind a data grid control to a **DataSet** using the following code.

```
DataSet newDataSet = webServiceProxy.GetDataSet();
this.dataGrid.SetDataBinding( newDataSet, "tableName" );
```

Sometimes you need to replace the contents of your dataset after all of the bindings with your controls have already been established. However, when you replace existing sets with new ones, the bindings all remain with the old data set.

Rather than manually recreating the data bindings with the new data source, you can use the **Merge** method of the **DataSet** class to bring the data from the new data set into the existing one, as shown in the following code example.

```
DataSet newDataSet = myService.GetDataSet();
this.dataSet1.Clear();
this.dataSet1.Merge( newDataSet );
```

Note: To avoid threading issues, you should only update bound data objects on the UI thread. For more information, see Chapter 6, "Using Multiple Threads."

Navigating Through a Collection of Data

If your data sources contain a collection of items, you can bind the data collection to your Windows Forms controls and navigate through the collection of data one item at a time. The user interface is automatically updated to reflect the current item in the collection.

You can bind to any collection object that supports the **IList** interface. When you bind to a collection of objects, you can allow the user to navigate through each item in the collection, automatically updating the user interface for each item. Many of the collection and complex data classes provided by the .NET Framework already support the **IList** interface, so you can easily bind to arrays or complex data such as data rows or data views. For example, any array object that is an instance of the **System.Array** class implements the **IList** interface by default, and so can be bound to the user interface. Many ADO.NET objects also support the **IList** interface, or a derivative of it, allowing these objects to be easily bound too. For example, the **DataViewManager**, **DataSet**, **DataTable**, **DataView**, and **DataColumn** classes all support data binding in this way.

Data sources that implement the **IList** interface are managed by the **CurrencyManager** object. This object maintains an index into the data collection though its **Position** property. The index is used to ensure that all controls bound to the data source read and write to the same item in the data collection.

If your form contains controls bound to multiple data sources, it will have multiple **CurrencyManager** objects, one for each distinct data source. The **BindingContext** object provides easy access to all **CurrencyManager** objects on the form. The following code example shows how to increment the current position within a collection of customers.

```
this.BindingContext[ dataset, "customers" ].Position += 1;
```

You should use the **Count** property on the **CurrencyManager** object as shown in the following code example to ensure that an invalid position is not set.

```
if ( this.BindingContext[ dataset, "customer" ].Position <
    ( this.BindingContext[ dataset, "customer" ].Count - 1 ) )
{
    this.BindingContext[ dataset, "customers" ].Position += 1;
}
```

The **CurrencyManager** object also supports a **PositionChanged** event. You can create a handler for this event so that you can update your user interface to reflect the current binding position. The following code example displays a label to show the current position and the total number of records.

```
this.BindingContext[ dataset, "customers" ].PositionChanged +=
        new EventHandler( this.BindingPositionChanged );
```

The method **BindingPositionChanged** is implemented as follows.

```
private void BindingPositionChanged( object sender, System.EventArgs e )
{
    positionLabel.Text = string.Format( "Record {0} of {1}",
        this.BindingContext[dsPubs1, "authors"].Position + 1,
        this.BindingContext[dsPubs1, "authors"].Count );
}
```

Custom Formatting and Data Type Conversion

You can provide custom formatting for data bound to a control using the **Format** and **Parse** events of the **Binding** class. These events allow you to control how data is displayed in the user interface and how data is taken from the user interface and parsed, so that the underlying data can be updated. These events can also be used to convert data types so that the source and destination data types are compatible.

Note: If the data type of the bound property on the control does not match the data type of the data in the data source, an exception is thrown. If you need to bind incompatible types, you should use the **Format** and **Parse** events on the **Binding** object.

The **Format** event occurs when data is read from the data source and displayed in the control, and when the data is read from the control and used to update the data source. When the data is read from the data source, the **Binding** object uses the **Format** event to display the formatted data in the control. When the data is read from the control and used to update the data source, the **Binding** object parses the data using the **Parse** event.

The **Format** and **Parse** events allow you to create custom formats for displaying data. For example, if the data in a table is of type **Decimal**, you can display the data in the local currency format by setting the **Value** property of the **ConvertEventArgs** object to the formatted value in the **Format** event. You must consequently format the displayed value in the **Parse** event.

The following code sample binds an order amount to a text box. The **Format** and **Parse** events are used to convert between the string type expected by the text box and the decimal types expected by the data source.

```
private void BindControl()
{
    Binding binding = new Binding( "Text", dataset,
"customers.custToOrders.OrderAmount" );
    // Add the delegates to the event.
    binding.Format += new ConvertEventHandler( DecimalToCurrencyString );
    binding.Parse  += new ConvertEventHandler( CurrencyStringToDecimal );
    text1.DataBindings.Add( binding );
}
private void DecimalToCurrencyString( object sender, ConvertEventArgs cevent )
{
    // The method converts only to string type. Test this using the DesiredType.
    if( cevent.DesiredType != typeof( string ) ) return;

    // Use the ToString method to format the value as currency ("c").
    cevent.Value = ((decimal)cevent.Value).ToString( "c" );
}
private void CurrencyStringToDecimal( object sender, ConvertEventArgs cevent )
{
    // The method converts back to decimal type only.
    if( cevent.DesiredType != typeof( decimal ) ) return;

    // Converts the string back to decimal using the static Parse method.
    cevent.Value = Decimal.Parse( cevent.Value.ToString(),
            NumberStyles.Currency, null );
}
```

Using the Model-View-Controller Pattern to Implement Data Validation

Binding a data structure to a user interface element allows the user to edit the data and ensures that these changes are then written back to the underlying data structure. Often, you will need to check the changes that the user makes to the data to ensure that the values entered are valid.

The **Format** and **Parse** events described in the previous section provide one way to intercept the changes the user makes to the data, so that the data can be checked for validity. However, this approach requires that the data validation logic be implemented together with the custom formatting code, typically at the form level. Implementing these two responsibilities together in the event handlers can make your code difficult to understand and maintain.

A more elegant approach is to design your code so that it uses the *Model-View-Controller* (MVC) pattern. The pattern provides natural separation of the various responsibilities involved with editing and changing data through data binding. You should implement custom formatting within the form that is responsible for presenting the data in a certain format, and then associate the validation rules with the data itself, so that the rules can be reused across multiple forms.

In the MVC pattern, the data itself is encapsulated in a model object. The view object is the Windows Forms control that the data is bound to. All changes to the model are handled by an intermediary controller object, which is responsible for providing access to the data and for controlling any changes made to the data through the view object. The controller object provides a natural location for validating changes made to the data, and all user interface validation logic should be implemented here.

Figure 2.5 depicts the structural relationship between the three objects in the *MVC* pattern.

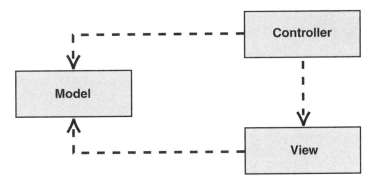

Figure 2.5
Objects in Model-View-Controller pattern

Using a controller object in this way has a number of advantages. You can configure a generic controller to provide custom validation rules, which are configurable at run time according to some contextual information (for example, the role of the user). Alternatively, you can provide a number of controller objects, with each controller object implementing specific validation rules, and then select the appropriate object at run time. Either way, because all validation logic is encapsulated in the controller object, the view and model objects do not need to change.

In addition to separating data, validation logic, and user interface controls, the MVC model gives you a simple way to automatically update the user interface when the underlying data changes. The controller object is responsible for notifying the user interface when changes to the data have occurred by some other programmatic means. Windows Forms data binding listens for events generated by the objects that are bound to the controls so that the user interface can automatically respond to changes made to the underlying data.

To implement automatic updates of the user interface, you should ensure that the controller implements a change notification event for each property that may change. Events should follow the naming convention *<property>***Changed**, where *<property>* is the name of the property. For example, if the controller supports a **Name** property, it should also support a **NameChanged** event. If the value of the name property changes, this event should be fired so Windows Forms data binding can handle it and update the user interface.

The following code example defines a **Customer** object, which implements a **Name** property. The **CustomerController** object handles the validation logic for a **Customer** object and supports a **Name** property, which in turn represents the **Name** property on the underlying **Customer** object. This controller fires an event whenever the name is changed.

```
public class Customer
{
    private string _name;
    public Customer( string name ) { _name = name; }
    public string Name
    {
        get { return _name; }
        set { _name = value; }
    }
}
public class CustomerController
{
    private Customer _customer = null;
    public event EventHandler NameChanged;
    public Customer( Customer customer )
    {
        this._customer = customer;
    }
    public string Name
    {
        get { return _customer.Name; }
        set
        {
            // TODO: Validate new name to make sure it is valid.
            _customer.Name = value;
            // Notify bound control of change.
            if ( NameChanged != null )
                NameChanged( this, EventArgs.Empty );
        }
    }
}
```

Note: Customer data source members need to be initialized when they are declared. In the preceding example, the **customer.Name** member needs to be initialized to an empty string. This is because the .NET Framework does not have a chance to interact with the object and set the default setting of an empty string before the data binding occurs. If the customer data source member is not initialized, the attempt to retrieve a value from an uninitialized variable causes a run-time exception.

In the following code example, the form has a **TextBox** object, **textbox1**, which needs to be bound to the customer's name. The code binds the **Text** property of the **TextBox** object to the **Name** property of the controller.

```
_customer = new Customer( "Kelly Blue" );
_controller = new CustomerController( _customer );
Binding binding = new Binding( "Text", _controller, "Name" );
textBox1.DataBindings.Add( binding );
```

If the name of the customer is changed (using the **Name** property on the controller), the **NameChanged** event is fired and the text box is automatically updated to reflect the new name value.

Updating the User Interface When the Underlying Data Changes

You can use Windows Forms data binding to automatically update the user interface when the corresponding underlying data changes. You do this by implementing a change notification event on the bound object. Change notification events are named according to the following convention.

```
public event EventHandler <propertyName>Changed;
```

So, for example, if you bind an object's **Name** property to the user interface and then that object's name changes as a result of some other processing, you can automatically update the user interface to reflect the new **Name** value by implementing the **NameChanged** event on the bound object.

Summary

There are many different considerations involved in determining how to handle data in your smart clients. You need to determine whether and how to cache your data, and how to handle data concurrency issues. You will often decide to use ADO.NET datasets to handle your data, and you will probably also decide to take advantage of the Windows Forms data binding functionality.

In many cases, read-only reference data and transient data needs to be dealt with differently. Because smart clients typically use both types of data, you need to determine the best way to handle each category of data in your application.

3

Getting Connected

By definition, smart clients need to connect to and communicate with other resources and form part of a distributed application. These resources can be client-side processes or components, or they may be network resources, such as a Web service.

This chapter examines the nature of communication between smart clients and other resources. It looks at the different technologies available for connecting and using resources in other processes, components, or remote services, and it discusses how to choose between them. Finally, it examines how best to design your smart clients to connect to resources.

Loosely Coupled and Tightly Coupled Systems

A client application can connect to and use components and services in other processes, both locally and on the network, in many different ways. It is useful to categorize the different approaches by how much coupling exists between the service and the client.

Coupling is the degree to which components (in a distributed system) depend on one another. The nature of coupling between clients and the services they communicate with can affect many aspects of the smart client design, including interoperability, offline capabilities, network communication performance, deployment, and maintenance considerations.

Tightly coupled systems often provide direct object-to-object communication, with the object on the client having detailed knowledge of the remote object. Such tight coupling can prevent independent updates to the client or the server. Because tightly coupled systems involve direct object-to-object communication, objects usually interact more frequently than in loosely coupled systems, which can cause performance and latency problems if the two objects are on separate computers and are separated by a network connection.

Loosely coupled systems are often message-based systems, with the client and the remote service unaware of how the other is implemented. Any communication between the client and service is dictated by the schema of the message. As long as the messages conform to the agreed-upon schema, the implementation of the client or service may be changed as required without fear of breaking the other.

Loosely coupled communication mechanisms offer a number of advantages over tightly coupled mechanisms, and they help to reduce the dependency between the client and the remote service. However, tight coupling often provides performance benefits and allows for a tighter integration between the client and the service, which may be required due to security or transactional requirements.

All distributed clients that communicate with remote services or components have some degree of coupling. You need to be aware of the different characteristics between the various loosely coupled and tightly coupled approaches so you can choose the right degree of coupling for your application.

Communication Options

When you design your smart client application, you can choose from a number of methods to connect it to other resources, including:

- Microsoft® .NET Enterprise Services
- Microsoft .NET remoting
- Microsoft Windows® Message Queuing (also known as MSMQ)
- Web services

.NET Enterprise Services

You can use .NET Enterprise Services to provide access to the COM+ service infrastructure of managed code components and applications. .NET components rely on COM+ to provide them with a number of component services, such as:

- Transaction support
- Role-based security
- Loosely coupled events
- Object pooling
- Queued components
- Just-in-time activation

A .NET component that uses COM+ services is known as a *serviced component*. Because your serviced components are hosted by a COM+ application, they must be accessible to that application. This introduces a number of registration and configuration requirements for the serviced component:

- The assembly must be derived from the **ServicedComponent** class in the **System.EnterpriseServices** namespace.

- The assembly must be strong-named.

- The assembly must be registered in the Microsoft Windows registry.

- Type library definitions for the assembly must be registered and installed into a specific COM+ application.

Assemblies that contain serviced components that are configured as out-of-process applications should be placed in the global assembly cache. Assemblies that contain serviced components configured as in-process libraries need not be placed in the global assembly cache, unless they are located in a different directory than the application. If you deploy multiple copies of the same version of a serviced component in this way, the COM+ catalog contains the global configuration for all instances of that component; it is not possible to configure them on a per-copy basis.

The following code example shows a component that requires a transaction and provides a method that writes data to a database within this transaction.

```
using System.EnterpriseServices;

[Transaction( TransactionOption.Required )]
public class CustomerAccount : ServicedComponent
{
[AutoComplete]
public bool UpdateCustomerName( int customerID, string customerName )
{
        // Updates the database, no need to call SetComplete.
        // Calls SetComplete automatically if no exception is thrown.
}
}
```

Serviced components can often register dynamically the first time they run. This type of registration is known as *lazy registration*. The first time a managed code application attempts to create an instance of a serviced component, the common language runtime (CLR) registers the assembly and the type library, and it configures the COM+ catalog. Registration occurs only once for a particular version of an assembly. Lazy registration allows you to deploy serviced components using Xcopy deployment and to work with serviced components during the development cycle without having to explicitly register them.

Lazy registration is the easiest method for registering your serviced components, but it works only if the process running them has administrative privileges. Also, any assembly that is marked as a COM+ server application requires explicit registration; dynamic registration does not work for unmanaged clients calling managed serviced components. In cases where the process that uses the serviced component does not have the required privileges for dynamic registration, you need to explicitly register the assembly containing the serviced component using the Regsvcs.exe tool provided with the .NET Framework.

Both lazy registration and Regsvcs.exe require administrative permissions on the client computers, so if your application includes serviced components, it cannot be deployed using no-touch deployment. For more details, see Chapter 7, "Deploying and Updating Smart Client Applications."

Serviced components can be hosted and accessed in a number of different ways. They can be hosted within an ASP.NET application and accessed through HTTP, or they can be accessed through SOAP or DCOM (the default setting). However, if the COM+ services need to flow with the call (for example, if you need the user's identity or a distributed transaction to flow from your application to the serviced component), DCOM is the only viable solution.

Note: If you use DCOM to communicate with COM+ applications, you need to deploy interop assemblies to the client computers, just as you would for traditional COM components.

Enterprise Services have many powerful component features that you can use in your smart client applications. However, you should usually use these features only within a single process, on a single client computer, or within a service boundary on the server. Enterprise Services are generally not the best choice for communication between a smart client application and services located on remote systems due to their tightly coupled nature. Use Enterprise Services if your smart client application needs to use COM+ services locally (for example, support for transactions, object pooling, or role-based security).

For more information about Enterprise Services, see "Writing Serviced Components" in *.NET Framework Developer's Guide* at *http://msdn.microsoft.com/library/default.asp?url= /library/en-us/cpguide/html/cpconwritingservicedcomponents.asp?frame=true*.

.NET Remoting

.NET remoting provides a flexible and extensible remote procedure call (RPC) mechanism by which .NET components can communicate. .NET remoting allows you to use a variety of communication protocols (such as HTTP or TCP), data encoding options (including XML, SOAP, and binary encoding) and various object activation models. It can provide a fast and efficient means of communication between objects.

.NET remoting allows you to call remote objects as though they are local by using a proxy object that appears to be the remote object. The .NET remoting infrastructure handles the interaction between the client code and the remote object through property and method calls, encoding the data to be passed between them and managing the creation and deletion of the remote target object.

The .NET remoting infrastructure requires that the client has detailed knowledge of the public methods and properties of the remote object to provide a client-side proxy. One way of ensuring that the client has this knowledge is to distribute a full implementation of the remote object to the client. However, it is much more efficient to factor in the public methods and properties to interface definitions and compile these interfaces into their own assembly. The interface assemblies can then be used by the client to provide a suitable proxy, and they can be used by the remote object to implement the necessary functionality. This technique also allows you to update the implementation of the remote objects without having to redistribute the full objects to the client.

You can manage the lifetime of remote objects in a number of ways. Objects can be created on demand to fulfill a single request, or you can control their lifetime more finely by using a lease mechanism, where the client maintains a lease on the remote object and the remote object is kept alive as long as the client wants to use it. .NET remoting can also guarantee that only one object instance exists for all clients. You can choose the lifetime for your application according to your requirements for state management and scalability.

The extensible infrastructure of .NET remoting allows you to create custom channels and sinks. Custom channels allow you to define the way in which data is transmitted over the network. For example, you can define a custom channel to implement a custom wire protocol. Custom sinks allow you to intercept and perform actions on the data as it is sent between objects. For example, you can define a custom sink to encrypt or compress the data before and after transmission.

.NET remoting has a powerful and extensible mechanism for communicating between objects. However, due to its tightly coupled nature, it may not be suitable for all situations. .NET remoting requires .NET-implemented objects on both the client and server; therefore, it is not suitable for situations in which interoperability between different environments is a requirement. .NET remoting is also not suitable in situations where tightly coupled RPC-style interaction between client and server is inappropriate. By default, .NET remoting does not provide any built-in mechanism for encryption or for passing the user's identity or a transaction between objects. For these situations, Enterprise Services should be used.

.NET remoting is a good choice, however, for communicating between objects in different processes on the client computer or within a service boundary, or for objects in different application domains.

For more details about using .NET remoting, see "An Introduction to Microsoft .NET Remoting Framework" at *http://msdn.microsoft.com/library/default.asp?url=/library/en-us /dndotnet/html/introremoting.asp?frame=true.*

For information about choosing between Web Services and Remoting, see "ASP.NET Web Services or Remoting: How to Choose" at *http://msdn.microsoft.com/library /default.asp?url=/library/en-us/dnbda/html/bdadotnetarch16.asp?frame=true.*

Message Queuing

With Microsoft Windows Message Queuing, it is easy for you to communicate with applications quickly and reliably by sending and receiving messages. Messaging provides you with guaranteed message delivery and a reliable way to carry out many business processes. Message Queuing provides a loosely coupled communication mechanism you can use within your smart client application. Message Queuing has the following features:

- **Guaranteed message delivery**. Message Queuing guarantees that messages are delivered despite the failure or absence of the remote system by storing messages in a queue until they can be delivered. Therefore, messages are considerably less affected by failures than are direct calls between components.

- **Message prioritization**. More urgent or important messages can be received before less important messages, which can help to guarantee adequate response time for critical applications.

Note: You can set message priority only for nontransactional messages.

- **Offline capabilities**. If messages cannot be delivered because the client is offline, they are stored in the outgoing queue and are delivered automatically when the client goes back online. Users can continue to perform operations when access to the destination queue is unavailable. In the meantime, additional operations can proceed as if the message had already been processed, because the message delivery is guaranteed when the network connection is restored.

- **Transactional messaging**. You send messages as part of a transaction. In this way, you can send several related messages or design your application to participate in a distributed transaction, and ensure that all messages are delivered in order and are delivered only once. If any errors occur within the transaction, the entire transaction is cancelled and no messages are sent.

- **Security**. The Message Queuing technology on which the **MessageQueue** component is based uses Windows security to secure access control, provide auditing, and encrypt and authenticate the messages your component sends and receives. Message Queuing messages can be encrypted on the wire to make them impermeable to packet sniffers. You can also prevent queues from receiving unencrypted messages.

Applications that use Message Queuing can send and read messages from queues by using the classes in the **System.Messaging** namespace. The **Message** class encapsulates a message to be sent to a queue, while the **MessageQueue** class provides access to a specific queue and its properties.

You need to install and configure Message Queuing on any computer that will use it. Message Queuing is available for Windows desktop operating systems and for Microsoft Windows CE .NET, allowing you to use it on mobile devices such as Pocket PC devices.

Message Queuing is a good choice for interacting with services that provide message-based access. You can use Message Queuing to communicate with other systems that have Message Queuing installed. Interoperability with other systems is limited, though you can use connectivity toolkits to communicate with other messaging systems such as MQSeries from IBM.

For more information about using Message Queuing, see "Message Queuing (MSMQ)" in the Microsoft Platform SDK documentation at *http://msdn.microsoft.com /library/default.asp?url=/library/en-us/msmq/msmq_overview_4ilh.asp?frame=true*.

For information about MSMQ-MQSeries bridge programming, see "Programming Considerations Using MSMQ-MQSeries Bridge Extensions" at *http://msdn.microsoft.com/library/default.asp?url=/library/en-us/his/htm /_sna_programming_considerations_using_msmq_mqseries_bridge_extensions_appl.asp*.

Web Services

A Web service is an application component that:

* Exposes useful functionality to other Web services and applications through standard Web service protocols.
* Provides a detailed description of its interfaces, allowing you to build client applications that communicate with it. The description is provided in an XML document called a Web Services Description Language (WSDL) document.
* Describes its messages by using an XML schema.

The SOAP-based XML messages of Web services can have explicit (structured and typed) parts or loosely defined parts (using arbitrary XML). This means that Web services can be either loosely coupled or tightly coupled and can be used to implement message-based or RPC-style systems, depending on the precise requirements of your environment.

You can use Web services to build modular applications within and across organizations in heterogeneous environments. These applications can be interoperable with a broad variety of implementations, platforms, and devices. Any system that can send XML over HTTP can use Web services. Because Web services are based on standards, systems written in different languages and on different platforms can use each other's services. This is often referred to as a service-oriented architecture.

The main standards used with Web services are HTTP, SOAP, UDDI, and WSDL. Web services are agnostic to transport protocols. However, HTTP is the most common mechanism for transporting SOAP messages. Therefore, Web services are well suited for applications that traverse networks and corporate firewalls, such as smart clients that need to communicate with services over the Internet.

A number of Web services standards are emerging to extend the functionality of Web services. Microsoft Web Services Enhancements (WSE) 2.0 supports emerging Web services standards such as WS-Security, WS-SecureConversation, WS-Trust, WS-Policy, WS-Addressing, WS-Referrals, and WS-Attachments and Direct Internet Message Encapsulation (DIME). WSE provides a programming model to implement various specifications that it supports. For more information, see "Web Service Enhancements (WSE)" at *http://msdn.microsoft.com/webservices/building/wse/default.aspx*.

For more information about SOAP, see "Understanding SOAP" at *http://msdn.microsoft.com/library/default.asp?url=/library/en-us/dnsoap/html /understandsoap.asp*.

For more information about WS-Security, see "Web Services Security Specifications Index Page" at *http://msdn.microsoft.com/library/default.asp?url=/library/en-us/dnglobspec /html/wssecurspecindex.asp*.

Web service communications can be coarse-grained, self-contained, and stateless. However, Web services are often very verbose compared to other forms of communication.

Web services are the best approach for building most smart client applications. The high degree of interoperability allows Web services to communicate with a wide range of applications. The use of widely adopted standards means that they can usually pass through network infrastructure and firewalls with minimal additional configuration (compared to other technologies that require proprietary ports to be opened). Strong support for Web services in the Microsoft Visual Studio® development system means that you can work with them in a single development environment.

Web services may not be appropriate in extremely high performance applications because they are verbose and contain relatively heavy message payloads compared to other messaging technologies such as .NET remoting and Message Queuing.

For more information about using and building Web services, see "XML Web Services Created Using ASP.NET and XML Web Service Clients" in *.NET Framework Developer's Guide* at *http://msdn.microsoft.com/library/default.asp?url=/library/en-us/cpguide/html /cpconaspnetbuildingwebservicesaspnetwebserviceclients.asp?frame=true*.

Choosing a Communication Option

Different communication options are appropriate in different situations. Table 3.1 summarizes the different options for getting connected.

Table 3.1: Smart Client Options

Option	Advantages	Disadvantages
Enterprise Services	Provides access to COM+ services Allows identity to flow with call	Requires serviced components to be installed at the client Suitable only for same process or computer
.NET remoting	Fast Pluggable Supports custom protocols	Requires .NET Framework to run Proprietary Cannot traverse firewalls without RPC ports open No security infrastructure
Message Queuing	Useful for communicating with messaging systems Secure Guaranteed message delivery	Requires Message Queuing to be configured on the client Does not integrate easily with other systems
Web services	Supports integration Extensible Strong industry support Clearly defined standards Vendor/language agnostic Secure	Verbose Performance slower than .NET remoting

As Table 3.1 illustrates, there are some situations in which Enterprise Services, NET remoting, and Message Queuing may be appropriate technologies for communication between smart clients and the connected resources. However, in most cases, Web services are the best mechanism for connecting smart client applications to services.

An architecture built around Web service communication can work well in both a connected and offline environment, with support for coarse-grained, stateless messages that are self-describing and self-contained. The reliance on Internet protocols allows for wide distribution of the client to anyone on the Internet.

Designing Connected Smart Client Applications

As you design your smart clients, there are a number of recommendations you should consider, including:

- Use coarse-grained, encapsulated messages.
- Avoid distributed ACID transactions.
- Avoid sending datasets across the network.
- Break up large datasets.
- Version your Web services and assemblies.

Use Coarse-Grained, Encapsulated Messages

Distributed network calls are expensive operations. You should not design your external interfaces in the same fine-grained way you would design local interfaces, or performance will suffer. To avoid message dependencies between messages, it is a good idea to build interfaces methods as self-contained functions. Doing so saves you from writing complex tracking reconciliation code to handle the failure of a message that depends on the successful completion of another.

Avoid Distributed ACID Transactions

Distributed ACID (atomic, consistent, isolated, durable) transactions are resource-intensive, with a lot of network traffic and a lot of interdependent system locks on pending local transactions. If your smart client or service is waiting for a reply and cannot continue until the reply is received, a distributed ACID transaction can block business processes.

The problems of distributed ACID transactions are exacerbated if your smart clients are likely to switch to offline mode without warning. In this case, a client may place a lock on data and go offline before the lock can be released at the server.

If you cannot avoid message dependency by breaking up your interfaces into single discrete messages, you have a number of options to deal with transactions and still avoid distributed ACID transactions:

- Submit tightly coupled messages to the server and have a transaction coordinator such as Microsoft BizTalk® Server handle message dependencies.
- Write transaction-compensating code yourself on the client or server. Use a communications protocol that the server can use to decide when to start a transaction and how to notify the client regarding the successful completion or failure of the transaction to be processed in its entirety.

Avoid Sending Datasets Across the Network

Datasets can be too big and verbose to use as a communication payload mechanism for sending data across many tiers. Instead, you should use data transfer objects (DTOs) to decrease the message payload to your external interfaces. For data changes, you should consider sending the only the changed data instead of the entire set of data.

For more information about DTOs see Chapter 2, "Handling Data."

Break Up Large Datasets

Large datasets can cause performance problems at the client if you try to display them all at the same time. Therefore, you should break them up into smaller datasets. Breaking up data in this way is known as *paging*. For example, instead of displaying the entire contents of a phone directory, you may choose to display one page at a time (for example, 20 records per screen, displayed alphabetically). If you design the client to use paging, you should ensure that the user interface is designed to make navigating between pages easy for the user.

This concept of breaking up large datasets also applies to communication with the server over the network. If you can break the data into manageable chunks, you can then load the required data on an as-needed basis, a technique known as *lazy loading*. In the phone directory example, only the data needed for the current operation would be loaded, reducing the impact on the application and on the network, and potentially making both more responsive.

To improve the user experience, you can use additional threads to perform background processing and communication with services in anticipation of upcoming user requests.

Although support for lazy loading may be an important aspect of your smart client application design, you should bear in mind the offline requirements of your application. Lazy loading of data that travels over the network may prevent your application from functioning offline as you hope.

Version Your Web Services and Assemblies

When you upgrade and release new versions of your smart client software to clients, you should create new versions of the assemblies. If you use versioned assemblies, and if you design your server services to support backward-compatible interfaces, you can support multiple versions of the client software. When releasing new versions of your Web services, you should differentiate them with a canonical naming convention. Alter the namespaces of each release so that they contain date information to make it clear what version of a Web service clients are communicating with.

For more details about handling multiple versions of assemblies, see Chapter 7, "Deploying and Updating Smart Client Applications."

Summary

Smart clients need to access resources, both local and remote, to function. How you handle this communication can be critical to your success in designing smart clients that are reliable and responsive to the user. Requirements such as performance, security, and flexibility affect what the appropriate connectivity choice is for your environment. Using the guidance in this chapter, you should determine which forms of connectivity are right for your smart clients, and then design your smart clients and the resources with which they communicate accordingly.

4

Occasionally Connected Smart Clients

We live in an increasingly connected world. However, in many cases we cannot rely on connectivity 100 percent of the time. Your users may travel, they may temporarily lose wireless connectivity, there may be latency or bandwidth problems, or you may need to take down parts of the network for maintenance. Even if users do have good network connectivity, your applications may not be able to access network resources all of the time. A requested service could be busy, down, or just temporarily unavailable.

An application is *occasionally* connected if at times it cannot interact with services or data over a network in a timely manner. If you can allow your users to be productive with their applications when they are offline, and still provide them with the benefits of a connected application when the connection is working, you can increase user productivity and efficiency and increase the usability of your applications.

One of the primary benefits of smart clients over Web-based applications is that they can allow users to continue working when the application cannot connect to network resources. Occasionally connected smart clients are capable of performing work when not connected to a network resource and then updating network resources in the background at a later time. The update may happen almost immediately, but sometimes it can happen days or even weeks later.

To given an application full occasionally connected capabilities, you need to provide an infrastructure that allows users to work when they have no connection to network resources. This infrastructure should include data caching, so that all required data is available on the client, and storage of the details of users' work, which can be used to synchronize the client and network resources when the user goes back online. The exact features and capabilities that your application needs to support occasionally connected operations depends on its connectivity, operational environment, and the functionality that the user expects when online and offline. However, all smart client applications should provide some sort of experience for the users when not connected to the network, even if the functionality is extremely limited. When designing and building your applications, you should always avoid generating error messages on the client because a server is not available.

This chapter looks at the issues that you face as you build applications with offline capabilities. It reviews different strategies for designing offline applications, discusses in detail design considerations, examines how to structure applications to use tasks, and looks at how your applications should handle data.

Common Occasionally Connected Scenarios

Occasionally connected smart clients are extremely useful in many common situations. Many offline scenarios involve the user explicitly disconnecting from the network and working without a network connection, for example:

- An insurance agent may need to create a new insurance policy while out of the office. He or she may be required to enter all the relevant data, calculate premiums, and issue policy details without being able to connect to the systems in the office.

- A sales representative may need to place a large order while on site with the customer, where the representative cannot connect to the server. He or she may need to consult price lists and catalog information, enter all order data, and provide estimates of delivery and discount levels without having to connect.

- A maintenance technician may require detailed technical information while attending to a service call at a client's site. The application helps him or her to diagnose the problem, provides technical documentation and details, and allows the technician to place an order for parts and to document his or her actions without having to connect.

Other offline scenarios involve intermittent or low quality connectivity, for example:

- Connectivity between customer call centers around the world and a corporate network may not be of sufficiently high quality to allow online usage at all times. The application should provide offline capabilities, including data caching, so that the usability of the application is maintained.

- Medical staff traveling with Tablet PCs may experience disruptions in network connectivity as they travel. When the application connects, it should synchronize data in the background, and should not wait for an explicit reconnect.

Occasionally connected smart clients should be designed to take maximum advantage of a connection when it is available, ensuring that both applications and data are as up to date as possible, without adversely affecting the performance of the application.

Occasionally Connected Design Strategies

There are two broad approaches to architecting occasionally connected smart client applications: *data-centric* and *service-oriented*.

Applications that use the data-centric strategy have a relational database management system (RDBMS) installed locally on the client, and use the built-in capabilities of the database system to propagate local data changes back to the server, handle the synchronization process, and detect and resolve any data conflicts.

Applications that use the service-oriented approach store information in messages and arrange those messages in queues while the client is offline. After the connection is reestablished, the queued messages are sent to the server for processing.

Figure 4.1 shows data-centric and service-oriented approaches.

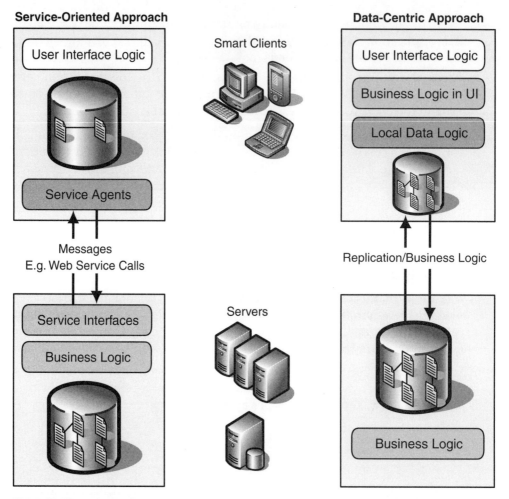

Figure 4.1

Service-oriented vs. data-centric approach to occasionally connected application design

This section examines both approaches in detail and explains when you should use each approach.

The Data-Centric Approach

When you use the data-centric approach, typically the server publishes the data and the client creates a subscription to the data it needs, so that it can copy that data to the local data store before the client goes offline. When the client is offline, it makes changes to the local data through calls to the local data store. When the client is back online, the data store propagates the changes made to the data on the client back to the server. Changes made to the data on the server may also be propagated back to the client. Any conflicts encountered during the merge phase are handled by conflict resolution rules specified on the server or the client, according to custom rules defined by the business analyst.

The process of merging changes between the client and server is known as *merge replication*. Changes can occur autonomously at both the client and the server, so ACID (atomic, consistent, isolate, durable) transactions are not used. Instead, when a merge is performed, all subscribers in the system use the data values held by the publisher.

The main advantage of the data-centric approach is that all change-tracking code is contained inside the relational database. Generally, this includes code for conflict detection at both the column and row level of the database, data validation code, and constraints. This means that you do not have to write your own change-tracking or conflict detection and resolution code, although you do need to be aware of the merge-replication scheme so that you can optimize your applications for data conflicts and data updates.

In the data-centric model, the database system handles synchronization; therefore, you do not need to implement all data synchronization functionality yourself. Users define which tables require data synchronization, and the database system allows the infrastructure to track changes and detect and resolve conflicts. You can extend this infrastructure to provide custom conflict resolution or avoidance through custom resolvers that use COM objects or Transact SQL (TSQL) stored procedures. Also, because there is a single data repository across the system, data convergence is guaranteed between a server and a client at the completion of synchronization.

There are, however, some disadvantages to a data-centric approach. The need for a local database on the client means that the approach may not be suitable in the following situations:

- If the application runs on a small device
- If a light-touch deployment mechanism is required
- If non-administrator users should be able to deploy the application

Microsoft provides database software that runs on the Windows® client, Windows Server™ and Pocket PC platforms, but it does not provide database software for SmartPhone devices.

Also, the tight coupling between the database on the server and the one on the client means that changes made to the database schema at the server have a direct impact on the client. This can make it difficult to manage database schema changes to the client or server.

With a large number of clients, there is a need to provide a manageable and scalable way to deploy distinct data sets. Merge replication supports dynamic filtering, which allows the administrator to define these offline datasets and deploy them in a scalable fashion. You should take advantage of the filtering mechanism provided by the database to reduce the amount of data to be sent between client and server, and to reduce the likelihood of conflicts.

There can be many benefits to using a local database to store and manipulate data locally. You can use the database to propagate local changes back to the server and to help handle synchronization issues.

You should use the data-centric approach when:

- You can deploy a database instance on the client.
- Your application can function in a two-tier environment.
- You can tightly couple the client to the server through data schema definitions and communication protocol.
- You want built-in change tracking and synchronization.
- You want to rely on the database to handle data reconciliation conflicts and minimize the amount of custom reconciliation code that needs to be written.
- You are not required to interact with multiple disparate services.
- Windows users are able to connect to a database directly through a local area network (LAN) or a virtual private network (VPN/IPSec). Applications written for the Pocket PC platform can synchronize HTTP through HTTPS.

Note: This guide does not cover the data-centric approach in depth. It is more fully described in many places, including the Microsoft SQL Server Books Online or MSDN. For more details on the data-centric approach, see "Merge Replication" at *http://msdn.microsoft.com/library/default.asp?url= /library/en-us/replsql/repltypes_6my6.asp*.

The Service-Oriented Approach

With the service-oriented approach, the client can interact with whatever services are required. Also, the client is focused on the service requests themselves, rather than on making direct changes to locally held data. The service requests may lead to state changes on the client or the server, but such changes are by-products of the service requests.

One advantage of the service-oriented strategy is that a local relational database is not required on the client. This means that the approach can be applied to many different client types, including those with a small amount of processing power, such as mobile phones.

A service-oriented approach is particularly appropriate when your application has to operate in an Internet and extranet environment. If your client operates outside the firewall and interacts with corporate services, by using a service-oriented strategy, you can avoid having to open up specific ports in the firewall, for example to enable direct database or Microsoft Message Queuing (MSMQ) access.

The loose coupling means that you can use different data schemas on the client than on the server, and transform the data at the client. In fact, the client and server do not need to be aware of each other. You can also update both the client and server components independently.

The main disadvantage of this approach is that you need to write more infrastructure code to facilitate the storing and forwarding of messages, as well as to detect when the application is online or offline. This can give you more flexibility in your design, but often means more work in creating your offline clients.

Note: The Smart Client Offline Application Block provides you with code that supports a service-oriented strategy for offline clients. You can use this block to detect when an application is on or offline and store and forward messages to a server for processing. For an overview of this application block, see *Smart Client Offline Application Block* at *http://msdn.microsoft.com/library /default.asp?url=/library/en-us/dnpag/html/offline.asp*.

The service-oriented approach is most suitable for smart clients that need to interact with a number of different services. Because the payload of the message is encapsulated, the transport layer can vary without affecting the contents of the message. For example, a message originally destined for a Web service could just as easily be sent to a service that consumed Message Queuing messages. The fact that the message is transport agnostic also allows for custom security implementations if required by the application.

You should use the service-oriented approach when:

- You want to decouple the client and server to allow independent versioning and deployment.

- You require more control and flexibility over data reconciliation issues.

- You have the developer expertise to write more advanced application infrastructure code.

- You require a lightweight client footprint.

- You are able to structure your application into a service-oriented architecture.

- You require specific business functionality (for example, custom business rules and processing, flexible reconciliation, and so on).

- You need control over the schema of data stored on the client and flexibility that might be different from the server.

- Your application interacts with multiple or disparate services (for example, multiple Web services or services through Message Queuing, Web services, or RPC mechanisms).

- You need a custom security scheme.

- Your application operates in an Internet or extranet environment.

While both the data-centric and service-oriented approaches are valid architectural approaches, many smart client applications are not able to support full relational database instances on the client. In such cases, you should adopt a service-oriented approach and ensure that you have the appropriate infrastructure in place to handle issues such as data caching and conflict detection and resolution.

For this reason, the remainder of this chapter focuses on the issues that smart client developers need to consider when implementing a service-oriented approach.

Designing Occasionally Connected Smart Client Applications Using a Service-Oriented Approach

As you design your occasionally connected smart clients using a service-oriented approach, there are a number of issues that you need to address. These include:

- Favoring asynchronous communication
- Minimizing complex network interactions
- Adding data caching capabilities
- Managing connections
- Designing a store-and-forward mechanism
- Managing data and business rule conflicts
- Interacting with create, read, update, delete (CRUD)–like Web services
- Using a task-based approach
- Handling dependencies

This section discusses these issues in more detail:

Favoring Asynchronous Communication

Applications use one of two methods of communication when interacting with data and services located on the network:

- **Synchronous communication**. The application is designed to expect a response before it continues processing (for example, synchronous RPC communication).
- **Asynchronous communication**. The application communicates by using a message bus or some other message-based transport, and expects a delay between the request and any response or expects no response at all.

Note: In this guide, synchronous communication refers to all communication that expects a response before processing can continue, even if the synchronous call is carried out on a separate background thread.

If you are designing a new smart client application, you should ensure that it primarily uses asynchronous communication when interacting with data and services located on the network. Applications that are architected to expect a delay between the request and a response are well-suited to occasionally connected use, as long as the application provides significant and useful functionality while waiting for a response and does not prevent a user from carrying on with his or her work if the response is delayed.

When the application is not connected to network resources, you can store requests locally and send them to the remote service when the application reconnects. In both the offline and online cases, because the application is not expecting an immediate response to a request, the user is not prevented from continuing to use the application and can continue working.

Applications that use synchronous communication, even on a background thread, are not well suited to be occasionally connected. You should therefore minimize the use of synchronous communications in your smart clients. If you are redesigning an application that uses synchronous communication to be a smart client, you should ensure that it adopts a more asynchronous communication model so that it can function offline. However, in many cases you can implement synchronous-like communication on top of an asynchronous infrastructure (known as the sync-on-async model) so that application design changes can be kept to a minimum.

Architecting your applications to use asynchronous communication can bring you benefits that go beyond occasionally connected use. Most applications designed for asynchronous communication are more flexible than those that use synchronous communications. For example, an asynchronous application can be shut down part way through a task without affecting the processing of requests or responses when it starts again.

In most cases, you do not need to implement both synchronous and asynchronous behavior in an application for online and offline usage. An asynchronous behavior is suitable for both online and offline use; requests are processed in near real time when the application is online.

Minimizing Complex Network Interactions

Occasionally connected smart clients should minimize or eliminate complex interactions with network-located data and services. When your application is offline, it may have to store requests and send them when the application reconnects, or it may need to wait a while for responses. Either way, the application does not immediately know whether a request will succeed or has succeeded.

To allow your application to continue working while offline, you must make certain assumptions about the success of network requests or changes to local data. Keeping track of these assumptions and the dependencies between service requests and data changes can be complex. To ease this burden, you should design your smart client applications around simple network interactions as much as possible.

Typically, requests that do not return any data (fire-and-forget requests) are not a problem for occasionally connected applications; the application can store the request and forward it when it reconnects. When the application is offline, it does not know if the call has succeeded; therefore, the application has to assume that the call succeeded. This assumption can influence subsequent processing.

If a request returns data that is required before the application can continue working, your application must use tentative or dummy values or function without the data. In this situation, you need to design the application to keep track of tentative and confirmed data, and design the user interface to make the user aware of data that is tentative or pending This allows the user or the application to make informed decisions based on the validity of the data and prevents problems with data conflicts and corruption later on.

In situations where the user completes a number of discrete units of work while offline, your application should allow each unit of work to succeed or fail on its own account. For example, in an application that lets the user enter order information, the application can let the user enter as many orders as required, but the application must make sure that one order does not depend on the success of another order.

It is relatively easy to ensure that there are no dependencies between units of work when the application has to make only one service request per unit of work. This allows your application to keep track of pending requests and to process them when it goes online. However, in some situations the user tasks are more complicated and multiple service requests have to be made to complete them. In these cases, the application must make sure that each request is consistent with the others so that it can maintain data integrity.

Adding Data Caching Capabilities

Your application needs to make sure that all of the data necessary for the user to continue working is available on the client when it goes offline. In some cases, your application should cache data on the client for performance reasons, but many times your application must cache additional data to allow for occasionally connected use. For example, volatile data may not have been cached for an application designed to be used online, but enabling the same application to work offline requires that the data be cached on the local computer. Both the client and server sides must be designed to account for data volatility so that they can handle updates and conflicts appropriately.

When an application is offline, you may choose not to delete out-of-date data from the application data cache and instead use the out-of-date data to allow the user to continue working. In other cases, the application may need to automatically delete the data from the cache to prevent the user from using it and causing problems at a later time. In the latter case, the application may cease to provide the required functionality until new data has been obtained through a synchronization process.

Refreshing data in the cache can occur in a number of ways, depending on the style and functionality of your application. For some applications, the cached data can be refreshed automatically when it expires, periodically according to some schedule, when the application performs a sync operation, or when the server changes the data and informs the application of the change. Other applications might allow the user to manually select data to be cached, allowing the user to examine or work on the data while offline.

Other data caching considerations also apply, such as security and data-handling constraints. These issues are not encountered solely in offline-capable applications and are described more fully in Chapter 2, "Handling Data."

Handling Changes to Reference Data

Reference data is data that changes infrequently. Typically, applications include a significant amount of this data. For example, in a customer record, the customer name changes infrequently. This type of data can easily be cached on the client, but sometimes your reference data will change and you must have a mechanism to propagate those changes to your smart clients.

You have two options for propagating the data: the push model and the pull model.

In the push model, the server proactively notifies the client and tries to push the data out. In the data-centric approach, this consists of the server data replicating the refreshed data on the client data stores. In the service-oriented approach, this could be a message containing the updated data. (This requires the client to implement an endpoint to which the server can connect.)

In the pull model, the client contacts the server for an update. The client may do this by checking the server on a regular basis or by examining metadata with the original data that states when the reference data expires. The client may even pull data from the server early (for example, a price list), and use it only when it becomes valid.

In some cases, you may choose to adopt a model where the server notifies the client that an update is available (for example, by sending an alert when the client connects), and the client then pulls the data from the server.

Managing Connections

As you are design your occasionally connected smart clients, you should consider the environment in which your application operates, both in terms of the available connectivity and the desired behavior of your application as this connectivity changes.

Some applications should be designed to operate for long periods of time (days or even weeks) without a connection. Others should be designed to expect a connection at all times, but have the ability to handle temporary disconnection gracefully. Some applications should provide only a subset of functionality when offline, while others should provide most of their functionality for offline usage.

While many occasionally connected scenarios involve the user explicitly disconnecting from the network and working without a connection, sometimes the application is offline without it being explicitly disconnected from the network. Your applications can be designed to deal with one or both of these scenarios.

Manual Connection Management

Your application can be designed to function when the user decides to work offline. The application must store all of the data that the user may need on the local computer. In this case, the user interacts with the application knowing that it is offline, and the application does not attempt to perform network operations until it is explicitly told to go online and perform a synchronization operation.

You may also include support for users to notify the application when they are using a connection that is of high connection cost or low bandwidth, such as a commercial wireless hotspot, a mobile phone connection, or a dial-up connection. In this case, the application may be designed to batch requests so that when a connection is formed, its use can be maximized.

Automatic Connection Management

Your application can be designed to dynamically adapt when changes to connectivity happen unexpectedly. These changes could include the following:

- **Intermittent connectivity**. Your application can be designed to adapt or handle gracefully those occasions when the network connection is temporarily lost. Some applications may temporarily suspend functionality until the application can go back online, whereas others must provide full functionality.

- **Varying connection quality**. Your application can be designed to anticipate that the network connection has low bandwidth or high latency, or may determine this dynamically and alter its behavior to suit its environment. If the connection quality deteriorates, the application may cache data more aggressively.

- **Varying service availability**. Your application can be designed to handle the unavailability of services it normally interacts with, and switch to its offline behavior. If the application interacts with more than one service and one of those services becomes unavailable, it may elect to consider all services as offline.

You can detect whether a smart client application has connectivity by using the wininet.dll. This is the same DLL that Microsoft Internet Explorer uses to determine whether users are connected to the Internet. The following code example shows how to call wininet.dll.

```
[DllImport("wininet.dll")]
private extern static bool InternetGetConnectedState( out int
        connectionDescription, int reservedValue ) ;

public bool IsConnected() {
  int connectionDescription = 0;
  return InternetGetConnectedState(out connectionDescription, 0);
}
```

Designing Store-and-Forward Mechanisms

If you design your application to use a service-oriented architecture, you must provide a store-and-forward mechanism. With store-and-forward, messages are created, stored, and eventually forwarded to their respective destinations. The most common implementation of store-and-forward is the message queue. This is the way in which message-oriented middleware products, such as Microsoft Message Queuing, work. As new messages are created, they are put into message queues and are forwarded to their destination addresses. While there are other store-and-forward alternatives (such as FTP or copying files between client and server), this guide focuses solely on the most common implementation: the message queue.

Your smart clients need a way of persisting messages when the smart client goes offline. If your application needs to create new messages when offline, your queue must have a way of persisting them for later updates with the server. The most obvious choice here is writing them to disk.

Your design needs to include functionality that ensures that messages are successfully delivered to their destination. Your design should take into account the following scenarios:

- **Lack of confirmation that a message was sent properly**. In general, you should not assume that a message was received at the server just because it has left a queue.

- **Loss of connectivity between the client and server**. In some cases, you must return a message from a queue because connectivity was lost between the client and the server.

- **Lack of acknowledgement from a service**. In this case, you may need to send an independent acknowledgement to inform the client that the information was received.

Your store-and-forward mechanism may also need to support additional functionality, such as message encryption, prioritization, locking, and synchronization.

Building and designing reliable messaging architectures is a complex task and requires considerable experience and expertise. For that reason, you should strongly consider commercial products such as Microsoft Message Queuing. However, Microsoft Message Queuing requires software on the client, which may not be an option for all smart clients.

Another option for message queue management is to use the Smart Client Offline Application Block, available at *http://msdn.microsoft.com/library/default.asp?url=/library /en-us/dnpag/html/offline-CH01.asp*.

This application block provides services and infrastructure that smart clients can use to provide offline capabilities to their applications. The block supports the store-and-forward approach to messaging using the message queue concept. By default, the block supports Message Queuing integration among other message persistence mechanisms (memory, isolated storage, and Microsoft SQL Server™ Desktop Engine [MSDE]).

Managing Data and Business Rule Conflicts

Changes that are made in an application in offline mode must be synchronized or reconciled with the server at some point. This raises the possibility of a conflict or other problem that the application, user, or administrator must resolve. When conflicts do occur, you must ensure that they are detected and resolved.

Unlike data conflicts, business rule conflicts do not occur because there is a conflict between two pieces of data, but because a business rule has been violated somewhere and needs to be corrected. Both data conflicts and business rule conflicts may need to be handled by either the client application or the user.

As an example of a business rule conflict, suppose that you have an order management application that caches a product catalog so that the user can enter orders into the system when offline. The orders are then forwarded to the server when the application is back online. If an order contains a product that was in the cached product catalog but has been discontinued by the time the application goes back online, when the order data is forwarded to the server it checks the order details and sees that the product has been discontinued. At this point, the application can inform the user that there is a problem with the order. If the product in question has been replaced or superseded, the system can give the user the ability to switch to a different product. This situation is not a data conflict because the data does not conflict with anything, but it is still incorrect and needs to be fixed.

Although business rule exceptions and data conflicts are different types of exceptions, they can most often be handled using the same basic approaches and infrastructure. This section discusses how to handle data and business rule conflicts in a smart client application.

Partitioning and Locking Data

Any system that allows multiple parties to access shared data has the potential for producing conflicts. As you design your smart client application, you must determine whether it partitions data and how it performs locking, because these factors help determine how likely conflicts are to occur in your application.

Data Partitioning

Data partitioning can be used in situations where different individuals have control over separate sections of data. For example, a sales representative may have a number of accounts assigned to him or her only. In this case, you can partition the data so that only that sales representative can change those accounts. Partitioning the data in this way allows users to make arbitrary changes to the data without fear of encountering data conflicts.

Designing your applications to use data partitioning is often very restrictive, and so is not a good solution in many cases. However, if data partitioning is practical for a specific application, you should strongly consider it, because it helps reduce the number of conflicts produced by your application.

Pessimistic Locking

Pessimistic locking is where the system uses mutually exclusive locks to ensure that only one party operates on system data at a time. All requests to data are serialized. For example, before going on the road, a salesperson may access a database and logically check out the customer accounts for customers in a certain geographic area. This check-out may require updating a spread sheet in the office and e-mailing others to update the account status. Now, when the salesperson is on the road, the rest of the sales staff understands that this salesperson has exclusive access to these customer files and is free to make whatever modifications necessary. When he or she returns to the office and synchronizes the new data with the server data, there should be no conflicts. After synchronizing the data, the salesperson releases the logical lock.

The main problem with pessimistic locking is that if multiple parties need to operate on the same data at the same time, they have to wait for the data to be available. For occasionally connected smart clients, data may be locked until a client comes online again, which could be a very long time. This makes pessimistic locking good in terms of data integrity because there is no possibility for conflicts, but bad in terms of concurrency.

In reality, pessimistic locking is only suitable for a few types of occasionally connected applications. In document management systems, for example, users may intentionally check out documents for a prolonged period of time while they work on them. However, as scalability and complexity increase, pessimistic locking becomes a less practical choice.

Optimistic Locking

Most occasionally connected smart client applications use optimistic locking, which allows multiple parties to access and operate on the same data concurrently, with the assumption that the changes made to the data between the various parties will not conflict. Optimistic locking allows high concurrency access to data, at the expense of reduced data integrity. If conflicts occur, you need a strategy for dealing with them.

In most offline scenarios you need to use optimistic locking. Therefore, you must expect data conflicts to occur, and you must reconcile them when they do.

Tracking Unconfirmed or Tentative Data

As your users work offline, any data they have changed is not confirmed as a change on the server. Only after the data has been merged with the server and there are no conflicts can the data truly be considered confirmed. It is important to keep track of unconfirmed data. When the data has been confirmed, it can be marked as such and used appropriately.

You may want to display unconfirmed data in your application's user interface in a different color or font so that the user is aware of its tentative nature. Generally, your applications should not allow data to be used in more than one task until the data has been confirmed. This prevents unconfirmed data from spilling over into other activities that require confirmed data. Using confirmed data is not a guarantee that there will not be a conflict, but at least the application will be aware that at one time the data was confirmed and has been subsequently changed by someone.

Handling Stale Data

Even if data has not changed, it can cease to be correct because it is no longer current. This data is known as *stale data*. As you design your smart-client applications, you need to determine how to deal with stale data and how to prevent your smart clients from using stale data. This is particularly important for occasionally connected smart clients because data may be current when a client first goes offline, but may become stale before a client goes online again. Additionally, data that is current on the client could be stale by the time it reaches the server. For example, a salesperson could create an order for various items on a Friday using valid data, but if he or she doesn't submit the order to the server until the following Monday, the cost of those items could have changed.

Note: If a service request is queued and is ready to be sent when your application goes back online, the chances that the request may encounter a data conflict or exception increase the longer that the request is queued. For example, if you queue a service request that contains an order for a number of items and you don't send the request for a long time, the items you order may be discontinued or sold out.

There are a number of techniques you can use to handle stale data. You can use metadata to describe the validity of data and show when the data will expire. This can prevent stale data being passed to the client.

At the server, you may choose to check any data from the client to determine if it is stale before you allow it to merge with the data on the server. If the data is stale, you could make sure that the client updates its reference data before resubmitting the data to the server.

The risk of stale data is greater with occasionally connected applications than with always connected applications. For this reason, your smart client applications will often perform additional validation steps to ensure that the data is valid. By adding extra validation into the system, you can also make sure your services are more tolerant of stale data, and in some cases you may be able to automatically handle the reconciliation on the server (that is, map the transaction to the new account).

Sometimes, stale messages are unavoidable. How you deal with stale data should be predicated on the rules of the business you are modeling. In some instances, stale data is acceptable. For example, suppose that an order is submitted for a particular item in an online catalog. The item has a catalog number, which has become stale because the online catalog changed. However, the item is still available and has not changed, the catalog number change has no effect on the system, and the correct order is generated.

On the other hand, if you are performing a monetary transaction between two accounts and one of the accounts has been closed, you cannot perform the transaction. Here the staleness of the data does matter.

A good general rule is to have business objects handle stale data situations for you. Your business objects can validate that data is current, and if it is stale, either do nothing, reconcile the stale data with equivalent current data, pass the information back to the client to be updated, or use business rules to automate an appropriate response.

Reconciliation of stale data may occur on the client, the server, or both. Handling reconciliation on the server allows your application to readily detect a conflict. Handling reconciliation on the client offloads some of the responsibility to the user or administrator who may be required to manually resolve any conflicts.

There is no one best way to handle stale data. Your business rules may dictate that the server is the best place to handle stale data if the client cannot resolve the conflict. If the server does not have enough information to automatically handle the situation, you may need to require that the client clean up its data before synchronizing with the server. Conversely, you may decide that stale data is perfectly fine for your application, in which case you have nothing to worry about.

Reconciling Conflicts

As you examine the data reconciliation requirements of your organization, you should consider the way your organization functions. In some cases, conflicts are unlikely to occur because different individuals are responsible for different elements of data. In other cases, conflicts will occur more frequently, and you must ensure that you have mechanisms in place to deal with them.

No matter what precautions you take, it is likely that a client will submit data to a network service that results in a business rule violation or data conflict. When a conflict does occur, the remote service should provide as much detail about the data conflict as possible. In some cases, it may be that the data conflict is not a major issue and can be handled automatically by the application or server. For example, imagine a customer relationship management (CRM) system where the user changes a customer's phone number. When the change is updated on the server, it is discovered that another user has also changed the phone number. You may choose to design your system so that the latest change always takes precedence, or you may want to send the conflict to an administrator. If the administrator knows who made the changes and when, he or she can then make a decision as to which one to keep. The important thing is that the server and application provide enough detailed information to enable automatic handling or to provide a user or administrator with enough information so that he or she can reconcile the conflict.

Data reconciliation can be a complicated and scenario-dependent problem. Every business and every application will have slightly different rules, requirements, and assumptions. However you have three general options for data reconciliation:

- Automatically reconciling data on the server
- Custom reconciliation on the client
- Third-party reconciliation

It is useful to look at each of these in turn.

Automatically Reconciling Data on the Server

In some cases, you can design your application so that the server uses business rules and automated processes to handle conflicts, without affecting the client. You can ensure that the latest change always takes precedence, merge the two elements of data, or employ more complex business logic.

Handling conflicts on the server is good for usability and saves the user from becoming deeply involved or inconvenienced by the reconciliation process. You should always keep the client informed about any reconciliation action taken; for example, by returning a reconciliation report to the client, explaining the conflict and how it was resolved. This allows the client to keep its local data consistent and informs the user of the reconciliation outcome.

For example, suppose that an application allows users to enter order information for items in a catalogue that is cached locally. If the user orders an item that has been discontinued but replaced with a newer but similar model, the order service may choose to replace the original item with the new one. The client is then informed of the change so that it can modify its local state appropriately.

Custom Reconciliation on the Client

In some cases, the client is the best place to perform reconciliation because it knows more about the context of the original request. The application may be able to resolve the conflict automatically. In other cases, the user or an administrator must determine how a conflict is to be resolved.

To allow effective client-side reconciliation, the service should send the client enough data to permit the client to make an intelligent decision about how the conflict can be resolved. The exact details of the conflict should be reported back to the client so that it or the user or an administrator can determine the best way to resolve the problem.

Third-Party Reconciliation

In some cases, you may want a third party to reconcile any data conflicts. For example, an administrator or supervisor can be required to reconcile important data conflicts. They could be the only users with the authority to determine the right course of action. In this case, the client needs to be informed that the decision is pending. The client may be able to continue by using tentative values, but often it will have to wait until the underlying conflict has been resolved. When the conflict is resolved, the client is informed. Alternatively, the client can poll periodically to determine the status, and then continue when it receives the reconciled value.

Interacting with CRUD-Like Web Services

Many Web services are created with Create, Read, Update, Delete (CRUD)–like interfaces. This section covers several strategies for creating occasionally connected applications that consume such services.

Create

Creating records should be a relatively simple task in a CRUD Web service, provided that you manage the creation of records correctly. The most important thing is to uniquely identify each record that is created. In most situations, you can do this by using a unique identifier as the primary key on your records. Then, even if two seemingly identical records are created on separate clients, the records will be seen as different when merge replication occurs.

Note: In some cases, you may not want the records to be treated as unique. In such cases, you can generate an exception when the two records conflict.

There are several methods you can use to create unique identifiers on an offline client. These include:

- Sending the record as a data transfer object (DTO) with no unique ID and allowing the server to assign the ID.
- Using a globally unique identifier (GUID) that the client can assign, such as a **System.Guid**.
- Assigning a temporary ID on the client and then substituting the real ID on the server.
- Assigning a block of unique IDs to each client.
- Using the user's name or ID to prefix all allocated IDs and handles, and incrementing them on the client so that they are globally unique by default.

Read

There are no data conflicts with read operations, because read operations are, by definition, read-only. However, problems can still occur with read operations in occasionally connected smart clients. You should cache any data that needs to be read on the client before it goes offline. This data can become stale before the client goes online again, leading to inaccurate data on the client and problems when synchronization occurs with the server. For more information about dealing with stale data, see "Handling Stale Data" earlier in this chapter.

Update

Data updates most frequently lead to data conflicts because multiple users may update the same data, leading to conflict when merge replication occurs. You can use a number of methods to minimize the occurrence of conflicts and then resolve them when they do occur. For more information, see "Managing Data and Business Rule Conflicts" earlier in this chapter.

Delete

Deleting a record is straightforward because a record can be deleted only once. Trying to delete the same record twice has no effect on the system. However, there are some things you should keep in mind when designing your application and Web service to handle deletions. First, you should mark the records as tentatively deleted on the client, and then queue the deletion requests on the server. This means that if the server is unable to delete the record for some reason, the deletion can be undone on the client.

As when you create records, you must also make sure that you refer to the records by using a unique identifier. This ensures that you always delete the correct record on the server.

Using a Task-Based Approach

The task-based approach uses an object to encapsulate a unit of work as a user task. The **Task** object is responsible for taking care of the necessary state, service, and user interface interactions that are required for the user to complete a specific task. The task-based approach is particularly useful when you design and build offline-capable smart client applications because it allows you to encapsulate the details of the offline behavior in a single place. This allows the user interface to focus on UI-related issues, rather than on processing logic. Typically, a single **Task** object encapsulates the functionality that the user associates with a single independent unit of work. The granularity and details of your tasks will depend on the exact application scenario. Some examples of tasks include:

- Entering order information
- Making changes to customers contact details
- Composing and sending e-mail
- Updating order status

For each of these tasks, a **Task** object is instantiated and is used to guide the user through the process, store all necessary state, interact with the user interface, and interact with any necessary services.

When an application is operating offline, it needs to queue up service requests and possibly make local state changes using tentative or unconfirmed values. During synchronization, the application needs to perform the actual service request and possibly make further local state changes to confirm the success of the service request. By encapsulating the details of this process within a single **Task** object — which puts the service request into the queue and tracks tentative and confirmed state changes — you can simplify the development of the application, insulate against implementation changes, and allow all tasks to be handled in a standard way. The **Task** object can provide detailed information about the state of the task through various properties and events, including:

- **Pending status**. Indicates that the task is pending synchronization.
- **Confirmed status**. Indicates that the task has been synchronized and confirmed as successful.
- **Conflict status**. Indicates that an error occurred during synchronization. Other properties will yield details of the conflict or error.
- **Completed**. Indicates percentage complete or flags the task as completed.
- **Task availability**. Some tasks will not be available when the application is online or offline, or if the task is part of a workflow or user interface process, it might not be available until a prerequisite task has been completed. This property can be bound to the enabled flags for menu items or toolbar buttons to prevent the user from initiating inappropriate tasks.

Another benefit of the task-based approach is that it focuses the application on the users and their tasks, which can result in a more intuitive application.

Handling Dependencies

If a user task involves more than one service request, the task needs to be handled very carefully so that the user can complete the entire task when offline. The challenge is that service requests are often dependent on each other. For example, suppose that you have an application that allows vacations to be booked for customers. To book a vacation, the application uses a number of services to perform each part of the overall task in the following sequence:

1. Reserve a car.
2. Reserve hotel accommodations.
3. Purchase the airline tickets.
4. Send e-mail confirmation.

Each of these services may be implemented by different systems, perhaps even by different companies. In a perfect world, each service request would succeed every time so that your user could reserve the car, hotel, and airline tickets successfully and the application could send e-mail notifying the client that the vacation was booked. However, not all service requests are successful, and your application must be able to resolve error conditions and manage business rules that affect how it handles the overall task. Writing code for this kind of task is extremely challenging because each part of the task (that is, each service request to a specific service) depends on another part of the task.

Dependencies can themselves depend on complex business logic, which further complicates the logic affecting the overall task. For example, your vacation booking application may allow the vacation to be booked if a car is unavailable, provided that the hotel and flights are reserved successfully. Dependencies between individual service requests can be both *forward* and *reverse* dependencies:

- **Forward dependencies**. If, during synchronization, the first request succeeds but a subsequent request fails, you may need to reverse the first request through a compensating transaction. This requirement can add significant complexity to the application.

- **Reverse dependencies**. If an application is operating offline and submits one service request as part of a multi-service request task, it has to assume that the request will be completed successfully so that it can queue subsequent requests and not block the user from completing the task. In this case, all subsequent requests are dependent on the success of the first request. If the first request fails during synchronization, the application must be aware that all subsequent requests need to be deleted or ignored.

Handling Dependencies at the Server

To reduce the complexities associated with dependencies between services requests, the Web service should provide a single service request per user task. This allows the user to complete a task that will be handled during the synchronization phase as a single atomic request to the Web service. A single atomic request eliminates the need to keep track of service request dependencies, which can significantly complicate the client- or server-side implementation of the application.

For example, instead of writing your service interfaces as three separate steps:

```
BookCar()
BookHotel()
BookAirlineTickets()
```

You can combine them into one step:

```
BookVacation( Car car, Hotel hotel, Tickets airlineTickets )
```

Combining steps in this manner means that, as far as the client is concerned, you now have one atomic interaction instead of three separate ones. In the example, the **BookVacation** Web service would be responsible for performing the necessary coordination between the elements that make up the service.

Handling Dependencies at the Client

You can also keep track of service request dependencies on the client. This approach provides significant flexibility, and allows the client to control the coordination between any number of services. However, this approach is difficult to develop and test. The task-based approach is a good way to keep track of service request dependencies on the client, and provides a way to encapsulate all of the necessary business logic and error handling in one place, which simplifies development and testing. (For more information about the task-based approach, see "Using a Task-Based Approach" earlier in this chapter.)

For example, the **Task** object used to book a vacation would know that it had to perform three service requests. It would implement the necessary business logic so that it could control the service requests appropriately if an error condition was encountered. If the **BookCar** service call failed, it could proceed with the **BookHotel** and **BookAirlineTickets** service calls. If the **BookAirlineTickets** service call failed, it would then be responsible for canceling any hotel or car reservation by creating a compensating transaction service request to each service. Figure 4.2 illustrates this task-based approach.

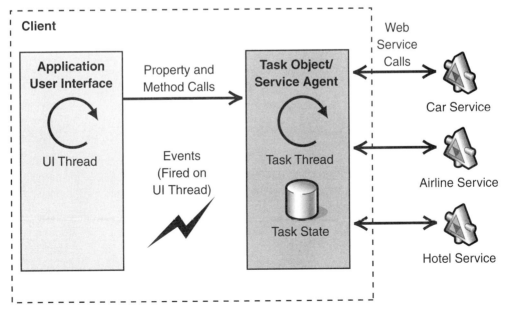

Figure 4.2

Task-based approach to service with interdependencies

Using Orchestration Middleware

Sometimes the dependencies and corresponding business rules in your applications are sufficiently complex to require some form of orchestration middleware, such as Microsoft BizTalk® Server, which coordinates the interactions between multiple Web services and a client application. Orchestration middleware is located in the middle tier and provides a facade Web service to interact with the smart client. The facade Web service presents an application-specific, appropriate interface to the client, which allows a single Web request per user task. When a service request is received, the orchestration service then processes the request by initiating and coordinating calls to the necessary Web services, possibly aggregating the results before returning them to the client. This approach provides a more scalable way to account for the interactions between multiple Web services. BizTalk also provides important services, such as data transformation and a business rules engine, that can help significantly when interacting with disparate Web services or legacy systems and in complex business scenarios. In addition, this approach provides important availability and reliability guarantees, which help to ensure consistency between multiple services. Figure 4.3 illustrates the use of orchestration middleware.

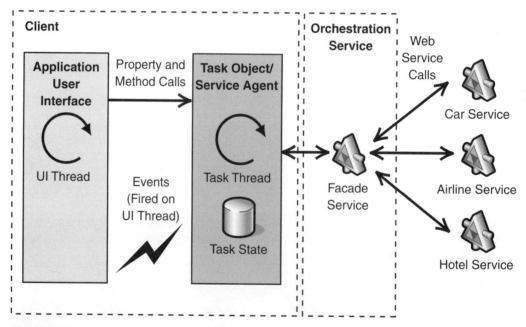

Figure 4.3

Orchestration middleware used to coordinate service dependencies

Summary

Smart clients need to operate efficiently when connected and disconnected from the network. As you design your smart clients, you need to ensure that they can function effectively in both situations, and transition seamlessly between the two.

There are two broad strategies for designing smart client communications: service-oriented and data-centric. When you have determined which of these to use, you need to make some fundamental design decisions to allow your smart clients to work offline. In most cases, the clients should be designed to use asynchronous communication and simple network interactions. Clients will need to cache data for use when offline, and you will need a method to handle data and business rule conflicts when the clients go back online. In many cases, offline clients allow users to perform a number of tasks that are dependent on one another. You will need to deal with these dependencies in the event that one of the tasks fails when it reaches the server. Your smart clients may also need to interact with CRUD-like Web services.

The task-based approach can dramatically simplify the process of taking applications offline. Consider implementing this approach in your smart clients; it can also provide you with an effective way of handling dependencies, both at the server and at the client.

5

Security Considerations

Smart clients are distributed applications that often span several different products and technologies. Managing security in these applications can be very challenging. At the server, you need to adopt an approach of securing the network, the server itself, and then the application. At the client, you should concentrate on using the security features of the platform (including the operating system and the Microsoft® .NET Framework), the privileged operations that the client code can perform (code access security), and the interactions with the server platform (domain) and server application.

Effective security depends on a defense-in-depth approach. As you secure your smart clients, it is very important to consider all aspects of security, including the following:

- **Authentication**. This uniquely identifies the user of the client application so that only approved users can access all or part of the application.

- **Authorization**. This determines the operations that the uniquely identified user can perform. These operations could be tasks or operations on resources to which the authenticated user is granted access.

- **Data validation**. This ensures that only appropriate and valid data is accepted by the application. If you permit any user input without first validating the data, an attacker can compromise the application by injecting malicious input.

- **Protecting sensitive data**. This means ensuring that sensitive data (such as passwords or confidential business data) stored and transmitted by the application is secure. Encrypting sensitive data ensures that data is not available in plain text; depending on choice of algorithm, it can also ensure that the information is not tampered with to maintain integrity.

- **Auditing and logging**. This involves keeping a record of events and user actions. You should consider logging key user actions or activities on the server or logging them securely on the client, because logs on client computers could be tampered or cleared.

- **Exception management**. This ensures that the application deals with exceptions appropriately, failing gracefully and returning user-friendly, non-sensitive information. Exception details can be logged to the event log or application log.

- **Change and configuration management**. This ensures that you keep track of the configuration of your IT environment and any changes that occur to it. Doing so allows you to see if unauthorized change occurs and determine the security implications of any authorized changes.

This chapter addresses in detail some of the key security challenges you will face as you design your smart client applications, specifically focusing on authentication, authorization, data validation, and securing sensitive data. The chapter also covers code access security, a key technology in the .NET Framework to manage security at code level rather than user level.

Another important aspect you need to consider when examining smart client security is how your smart client is deployed. For more information about the security issues affecting deployment, see Chapter 7, "Deploying and Updating Smart Client Applications."

Note: Any code you use in your application should be analyzed with FxCop. This tool allows you to check managed code assemblies for conformance to the .NET Framework design guidelines, including a base level of security compliance. FxCop can be downloaded off the GotDotNet site at *http://www.gotdotnet.com/team/fxcop/*.

Authentication

Authentication is the process of uniquely identifying a user by verifying his or her credentials. User authentication may be required when the user attempts to run or install the application or when the application makes a connection to a remote service or accesses locally held data.

This section examines some authentication scenarios common to smart clients, covers some of the different ways in which you can make authenticated network calls, and discusses how to gather user credentials and validate those credentials when offline.

Smart Client Authentication Scenarios

Depending on the style and functionality of your smart client application, you may need to authenticate the user at one or more points during the user's interaction with the application. There are four points at which you might choose to authenticate the user:

- When the application is installed
- When the application is run
- When the user accesses sensitive locally held data
- When the user accesses external services over the network

Installation

If your application is centrally deployed (for example, using no-touch deployment), you may need to secure the application on the Web server so that it can be installed only by authorized users. These users must first be authenticated by the Web server, which checks to see if they are authorized to access the application and download it to their client computers.

Securing access to a no-touch deployed smart client application is similar to securing any other Web server located artifact, such as a Web page. Microsoft Internet Information Services (IIS) provides a number of authentication mechanisms, such as Integrated Windows, digest, or basic authentication.

Note: Digest and basic authentication are not suitable if you are using no-touch deployment and your application uses a configuration file to store its configuration settings, because the configuration file cannot be downloaded automatically by the .NET Framework using these mechanisms.

After you select the appropriate authentication mechanism, and IIS can identify the user from his or her credentials, you can secure the application and its dependent assemblies by setting file permissions on the application and assembly files. To ease the management of large numbers of users, you may consider providing access to a Microsoft Windows® group (for instance, SmartClientAppUsers) and putting individual users into that group.

All users that you need to authenticate must have a Windows identity on the server so that IIS can secure access to the application and its assemblies, but they do not necessarily need to be logged on to their client computers using this identity. If the user's logon account is not known on the server side, the user is prompted for a user name and password when he or she clicks the link to the application's executable file.

If you use Integrated Windows authentication, the credentials of the logged on user are automatically used to try and gain access to the application. This allows for seamless but secure access when the user is logged on with an identity common to both the client and server.

Authenticated Application Access

Authenticating users to install an application ensures that only authenticated and authorized users are able to run your application from a central location. However, because the application and its dependent artifacts may have been cached on the client computer, you cannot rely on this mechanism to authenticate the user every time the application runs. In this case, or when the application is intentionally deployed locally, you need to carefully consider how user authentication is to be carried out by your application. You may need to authenticate users each time they run the application, particularly if your application provides sensitive functionality, or if you need to be able to revoke a user's authorization to run the application at any time.

In cases where the user is logged on to the client computer using an identity that is common to both the client and server, you may be able to rely on the fact that the user was able to log on to the client computer as sufficient authentication to run the application. This approach allows you to use the Microsoft Windows operating system to provide user authentication, obviating the need to implement it in your code. Also, because Windows can cache user credentials when offline, you do not need to cache them yourself.

For client computers for which you do not have any control over user access, such as those outside your organization's intranet, you may need to adopt a custom authentication mechanism to gather the user's credentials and authenticate them against a remote security authority. If the application is capable of operating offline, you need to cache valid credentials on the client so you can reauthenticate the user against them when he or she starts the application. You should enforce online reauthentication periodically to prevent unlimited use of such applications.

Authenticated Local Data Access

A smart client application often caches data that it has obtained from a remote service (for example, to improve responsiveness or to allow offline capabilities). If the data is sensitive, you might need to consider authenticating the user before granting access to it. In this case, you might choose to allow unauthenticated users to run the application but require users to be fully authenticated and authorized before giving them access to sensitive data.

Note: It is important to ensure that only data that the user is authorized to access be cached locally. If the data is sensitive, you also need to ensure that adequate measures are taken to guarantee its security. For details, see "Handling Sensitive Data" later in this chapter.

Locally held data should be held in a secure location and encrypted. Regardless of how users are authenticated, you typically want to use their credentials in some way to access and decrypt the data.

You may be able to use the default credentials that were used to log on to the client computer, or you may need to obtain custom credentials to authenticate the user against a remote security authority. The former possibility is most suitable for applications running in an intranet situation, while the latter is suitable for applications running in an Internet or extranet situation where the users are typically not in the same domain as the remote services they access. One of the benefits of using Integrated Windows authentication is that the operating system authenticates the user, secures the application and local data, and can cache the user's credentials when the user is offline.

For more information about caching sensitive data locally, see "Handing Sensitive Data" later in this chapter.

Authenticated Network Access

You might choose to enable anonymous access to the application and allow any user to download and run it. However, after the application is running on the client, it often needs to access remote services over the network, such as a Web service, to obtain data and services.

Access to network data and services often needs to be secured to prevent unauthorized access. There are many ways in which you might secure remote service access, but usually you need to pass the user's credentials to the remote service so that it can perform user authentication.

Authenticating users when they access remote services over the network is an important issue. Some of the options for ensuring authenticated network service calls are described more fully in "Network Access Authentication Types" later in this chapter.

Choosing the Right Authentication Model

The previous section described the four stages at which you might choose to authenticate the user. You might choose to authenticate the user at one or more of these points, depending on the nature of your application and its functionality. It is important to choose the right point to help ensure that your application and data remain secure, while minimizing any impact on the usability of your application.

If your application is centrally deployed (for example, if it is deployed using no-touch deployment or is deployed to a file share), you might choose to restrict access to users who are authorized. If you want your application to be available to anyone who wants to use it, authenticating the user when the application is installed is not required.

Client computers are generally not physically secure and may even be publicly accessible. If this is the case, and your application provides sensitive functionality, you often need to authenticate the user when the application runs. If your application provides generic functionality that is available to anonymous users, you do not need to authenticate the user at this point. However, you might choose to provide a portion of your application's functionality to anonymous users but require authentication before allowing them to access more restricted functionality.

Securing access to locally held sensitive data is critically important. If your application is deployed to a device that is not physically secure or is accessible to the public, sensitive data should be secured and should be accessible only by authenticated and authorized users. Your application might provide generic functionality to anonymous users but require user authentication when users try to access the sensitive data.

Using Integrated Windows authentication also has benefits when the application runs offline. In this case, Windows caches the user credentials so that the user is authenticated when he or she logs on to the offline client computer. This behavior obviates the need for your client to authenticate the user if you need user authentication when the application runs or accesses locally held sensitive data.

Network Access Authentication Types

There are many different technologies that you can use to authenticate users when accessing remote services, including:

- Integrated Windows authentication
- HTTP basic authentication
- HTTP digest authentication
- Certificate-based authentication
- Web Services Enhancements (WSE)–based authentication
- Custom authentication

Integrated Windows Authentication

With Integrated Windows authentication, the user is authenticated by logging on to his or her computer using a valid Windows account. The credentials could be a local account (an account local to the computer) or a domain account (a valid member of a Windows domain). The identity established during logon can be transparently used by your application to access resources for the entire duration of the user's session. This means that your applications can provide seamless access to network resources, such as Web services, in a secure way without having to prompt the user for additional, or repeated, credentials.

Note: Access to the network resources is seamless only if the network resources also use Integrated Windows authentication.

Integrated Windows authentication uses one of two authentication protocols: Kerberos or NTLM. These technologies do not pass a user name and password combination across the network to authenticate or validate the user. As a result, your application or infrastructure does not have to provide additional security to manage credentials during transit.

Client applications that rely on Windows security use an implementation of the **IIdentity** interface named **WindowsIdentity**.

Note: The .NET Framework also provides the closely related **IPrincipal** interface. For more details about **IIdentity** and **IPrincipal** interfaces, see "Authorization" later in this chapter.

Web Services that Use Integrated Windows Authentication

For Web services that are configured for Integrated Windows authentication, the client application can supply currently logged-on user credentials for authentication purposes before making Web service calls. When you add a reference to a Web service in your application from within the Microsoft Visual Studio® .NET development system, a proxy class is automatically generated and added to your project to programmatically access the Web service. The following code illustrates how to set the credentials of the user who is currently logged on.

```
MyService service = new MyService();  // A proxy for a web service.
service.Credentials = CredentialCache.DefaultCredentials;
service.SomeServiceMethod();           // Call the web service.
```

In this case, the **DefaultCredentials** uses the security context in which the application is running, which is usually the Windows credentials (user name, password, and domain) of the user running the application.

HTTP Basic Authentication

HTTP basic authentication is provided by IIS. With basic authentication, IIS prompts users for a valid Windows account and password. This combination is passed from the client to the server as encoded plain text and is used to authenticate the user at the Web server.

Note: To secure basic authentication, you need to secure the communication channel between the client and the server (for example, by enabling Secure Sockets Layer [SSL] on the server) to ensure that the user name/password combination is encrypted and cannot be tampered with or intercepted when in transit. You also need to secure the passwords located on the server. However, SSL can secure communication only between two defined endpoints. If you require secure communication between more than two endpoints, you need to use message-based security.

Web Services that Use Basic Authentication

For a client application interacting with a Web service configured for basic authentication, the client can accept valid user credentials using a logon dialog box and use it for authentication. The following code illustrates how to set the credentials of the user to the Web service proxy expecting basic authentication.

```
CredentialCache cache = new CredentialCache();
cache.Add( new Uri( service.Url ),     // Web service URL.
   "Basic",                 // Basic Authentication.
   new NetworkCredential( userName, password, domain ) );
service.Credentials = cache;
```

In this case, **userName**, **password**, and **domain** are accepted as part of the logon dialog box.

HTTP Digest Authentication

HTTP digest authentication offers the same features as HTTP basic authentication but involves a different way of transmitting the authentication credentials. The authentication credentials are converted in a one-way process referred to as *hashing*. The result of this process is called a *hash*, or *message digest*, and it is not feasible to decrypt it using current technologies.

Digest authentication occurs in the following way:

1. The server sends the browser certain information that will be used in the authentication process.
2. The browser adds this information to its user name and password, along with some other information, and hashes it. The additional information helps to prevent someone from copying the hash value and using it over again.
3. The resulting hash is sent over the network to the server along with the additional information in clear text.
4. The server adds the additional information to a plain text copy it has of the client's password and hashes all of the information.
5. The server compares the hash value it received with the one it just made.
6. Access is granted only if the two values are identical.

The additional information is added to the password before hashing so that nobody can capture the password hash and use it to impersonate the true client. Values are added that help to identify the client, the client's computer, and the realm, or domain, the client belongs to. A time stamp is also added to prevent a client from using a password after the password has been revoked.

Because digest authentication sends the password over the network in hashed form, it is clearly preferable to basic authentication, especially if you use basic authentication without encrypting the communication channel. Therefore, you should use digest authentication instead of basic authentication whenever possible.

Note: As with basic authentication, digest authentication completes only if the domain server for which a request is made has a plain-text copy of the requesting user's password. Because the domain controller has plain-text copies of passwords, you must ensure that this server is secured from both physical and network attacks.

Certificate-based Authentication

Certificates can enable client and server applications to authenticate each other or to establish a secure connection using digital keys installed on the computer. The client application can use client certificates to identify itself to the server, just as the server can identify itself to the client using a server certificate. A mutually trusted third party, called a certificate authority, can confirm the identity of the certificates. Client certificates can be mapped to Microsoft Windows accounts in Microsoft Active Directory® directory service.

You can set up a site so that users without certificates are logged on as guests, but users with certificates are logged on as the user to which his or her certificate maps. You can then customize the site based on the certificate.

If you need to authenticate individual users, you can use a technique known as one-to-one mapping where a certificate is mapped to an individual account. If you need to authenticate all of the users from a particular group or organization, you can use many-to-one mapping where, for example, any certificate containing a common company name is mapped to a single account.

In certificate-based authentication, client applications use certificates that can be authenticated by Web services. In this case, the client application digitally signs the SOAP messages using X.509 certificates to ensure that the message is from a trusted source and is not altered during transit before it reaches the designated Web service.

One major consideration of certificate-based authentication is how to manage situations when a certificate should no longer be valid. For example, if an employee uses a certificate to be authenticated and that employee is then dismissed, the certificate should no longer allow the user to access resources. Therefore, it is important that your certificate security infrastructure includes the administration of certificate revocation lists. These lists are present on the server and should be checked each time the client connects to a network resource.

Server-based revocation lists cannot be checked when a smart client goes offline, so there is potential for a user to access resources locally on the client that he or she should not be able to access at the server. To help get around this problem, you may choose to have relatively short lease times on your client certificates. Short lease times force the client to regularly connect to a certificate server and verify that the certificate has not been revoked prior to renewing the lease and allowing connection to the server side of the application.

For more information, see "About Certificates" at *http://www.microsoft.com/resources /documentation/windowsserv/2003/standard/proddocs/en-us/sec_auth_certabout.asp*.

WSE-based Authentication

You can programmatically sign the SOAP messages to a Web service using Web Services Enhancements version 2.0. WSE 2.0 is an implementation that supports emerging Web services standards such as WS-Security, WS-SecureConversation, WS-Trust, WS-Policy, WS-Addressing, WS-Referral, and WS-Attachments and Direct Internet Message Encapsulation (DIME). WSE provides a programming model to implement various specifications that it supports.

Client applications that use WSE can use one of the **Find** methods (for example, **FindCertificateByHash** or **FindCertificateByKeyIdentifier**) on the **X509CertificateStore** class to programmatically select a certificate from the store, create a digital signature using the certificate, add it to the WS-Security SOAP header, and call the Web service. Alternatively, the client application can also open the certificate store of the currently logged-on user as shown in the following code example.

```
X509CertificateStore store;
store = X509CertificateStore.CurrentUserStore( X509CertificateStore.MyStore );
bool open = store.OpenRead();
```

For more information, see "Web Services Enhancements" at *http://msdn.microsoft.com /webservices/building/wse/default.aspx*.

For more information about using client certificates, see "Signing a SOAP Message Using an X.509 Certificate" in the WSE 2.0 documentation.

Custom Authentication

In some cases, the standard authentication options provided by Windows are not appropriate for your applications, and you will need to design your own form of authentication. Fortunately, the .NET Framework provides options to help you design a custom authentication solution.

The .NET Framework supports an implementation of **IIdentity**, called **GenericIdentity**. You can use **GenericIdentity**, or create your own custom identity class. Designing a custom authentication solution can be difficult, because you have to take your own steps to ensure that the method is secure. You may also have to maintain a separate store for your identities.

Gathering and Validating User Credentials

Whatever form of authentication you use, you need to gather user credentials that can then be validated. For users that are already logged on using Integrated Windows authentication, you may just need to gather the existing credentials, and for a custom authentication solution, you may need to gather credentials securely through your own logon dialog box.

Note: Do not store user credentials in your code for longer than is necessary. In particular, do not store credentials in global variables, which provide access to them through publicly accessible methods or properties, and do not save them to disk.

Gathering Currently Logged-On User Credentials

If you are using Integrated Windows authentication, your users log on at the start of their Windows session. Your applications can then use this information to ensure that they have the appropriate credentials to run.

The following code demonstrates the basic functionality.

```
using System.Security.Principal;

// Get principal of the currently logged in user.
WindowsPrincipal wp = new WindowsPrincipal( WindowsIdentity.GetCurrent() );

// Display the current user name.
label1.Text = "User:" + wp.Identity.Name;

// Determine if user is part of a windows group.
if( wp.IsInRole( "YourDomain\\YourWindowsGroup" ) )
{
    // Is a member.
}
else
{
    // Is not a member.
}
```

Gathering User Credentials Using a Logon Dialog Box

If you are designing your own logon dialog box to accept credentials from the user, you need to take a number of measures to ensure that you meet the security requirements of your organization (such as enforcing strong password policy and having passwords expire at periodic intervals). Consider the following guidelines when you design your logon dialog box:

- **Do not blindly trust user input**. If you do so, a malicious user can compromise your application. For example, an application that uses input with no validation to dynamically construct SQL code can be vulnerable to SQL injection attacks.

- **Check for type, format, or range of input data**. Consider using regular expressions to do these checks. Using regular expressions enables you to check for type (for example, string or integer), format (for example, enforcing password policy requirements such as use of numbers, special characters, and a mix of lowercase and uppercase characters), and range (for example, a user name with a minimum of 6 characters and maximum of 25 characters).

  The following code example enforces a password between 8 and 10 characters long with a combination of uppercase, lowercase, and numeric characters.

  ```
  // Validate the user supplied password.
  if( !Regex.Match( textBox1.Text,
          @"^(?=.*\d)(?=.*[a-z])(?=.*[A-Z]).{8,10}$",
          RegexOptions.None ).Success )
  {
      // Invalid email address.
  }
  ```

- **Do mask the password field**. When designing a dialog box with a password field text box, ensure that the **PasswordChar** property is set to a character that is displayed when text is entered in the control, as shown in the following example.

  ```
  // The password character is set to asterisk.
  textBox1.PasswordChar = '*';
  ```

Authentication Guidelines

When designing authentication for your applications, you should consider the following guidelines:

- Determine where authentication needs to occur during the user's interaction with your application.
- Consider using Integrated Windows authentication to authenticate users as they log on to the client and before they can access your application, its data, and any remote service.
- If your application is centrally deployed and you need to restrict access to only authorized users, authenticate users when the application runs using one of the authentication mechanisms provided by IIS.
- If your application provides sensitive functionality or access to sensitive locally held data, ensure that users are properly authenticated before allowing access.
- If your application requires custom authentication, ensure your application enforces a strong user name and password policy. As a general practice, you should require a minimum of 8 characters and a mixture of uppercase and lowercase characters, numbers, and special characters.
- Require user authentication for access to remote services over the network if they provide sensitive functionality or access to sensitive data.
- Ensure that user credentials are not transmitted unprotected over the network. Some forms of authentication avoid passing user credentials over the network at all, but if they must be transmitted, you should ensure that they are encrypted, or sent over a secure connection.

For more information, see "Authentication" in "Chapter 4 — Design Guidelines for Secure Web Applications" of *Improving Web Application Security: Threats and Countermeasures* at *http://msdn.microsoft.com/library/default.asp?url=/library/en-us /dnnetsec/html/THCMCh04.asp*.

Authorization

After users are authenticated, you can determine what they have access to within the system by using authorization. Authorization is confirmation that an authenticated user has permission to perform an operation. Authorization governs the resources (for example, files and databases) that an authenticated user can access and the operations (for example, changing passwords or deleting files) that an authenticated user can perform. Users who are not authenticated (that is, anonymous users) are not able to be specifically authorized and need to be assigned a default set of permissions.

A number of factors determine exactly how you perform authorization in your environment. You need to determine whether to manage authorization based on application functionality or system resources. You need to decide whether to perform fine-grained authorization within methods or to perform checks at the method level. You also need to determine where the user information required for authorization is stored (for example, in Active Directory or a Microsoft SQL Server™ database). If you are going to allow your smart clients to work offline, you need a strategy for authorization of offline clients.

The .NET Framework provides the **IPrincipal** interface, which is used in conjunction with the **IIdentity** interface to define properties and methods to manage the security context of running code. Two implementations of this interface are also provided: **WindowsPrincipal** and **GenericPrincipal**. Client applications that use Integrated Windows authentication use **WindowsPrincipal**, whereas client applications that use custom authentication use **GenericPrincipal**.

Types of Authorization

Two methods of authorization are commonly used in the Windows operating system: resource-based authorization and role-based authorization. Resource-based authorization relies on access control lists (ACLs), and role-based authorization performs authorization based on user roles.

Resource-based Authorization

For resource-based authorization, you can attach discretionary access control lists (DACLs) to securable objects. The system then makes access decisions by comparing the group memberships in a token to the contents of the ACL to determine whether the user has the requested access. The ACL model is ideal for many types of applications. However, it is not appropriate for all situations. For example, you may need to make access decisions based on business logic or on nonpersistent objects that are created when needed.

Role-based Authorization

Role-based authorization allows you to associate users and groups with the permissions that they need to do their jobs. When a user or group is added to a role, the user or group automatically inherits the various security permissions. These could be permissions to perform actions or to access various resources. Figure 5.1 shows the relationship between roles and permissions in role-based authorization.

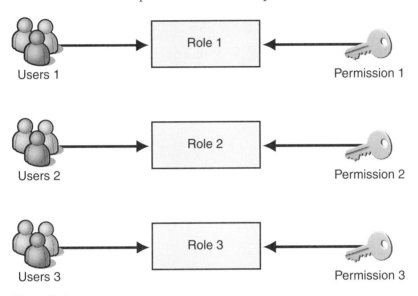

Figure 5.1
Role-based authorization

In Microsoft Windows 2000 Server Service Pack 4 (SP4) and Windows Server™ 2003 operating system, role-based authorization is generally administered using Authorization Manager. Authorization Manager is a set of COM-based run-time interfaces, along with a Microsoft Management Console (MMC) snap-in for configuration. Developers can use Authorization Manager to ensure that applications can manage and verify client requests to perform application operations, and application administrators can use it to manage user roles and permissions. With Authorization Manager, you can aggregate low-level operations into groups called Tasks and manage authorization at that level. It also allows you to run custom authorization logic before and after authorization.

One significant advantage of Authorization Manager is that it further abstracts the authorization store from the application requiring authorization, meaning that developers can always communicate with Authorization Manager, regardless of whether the store is in Active Directory or is file-based.

Adding Authorization Capabilities to Your Application

The .NET Framework provides a number of options for adding authorization capabilities to your application. These include:

- Performing declarative demands using the **PrincipalPermissionAttribute**
- Performing imperative demands using the **PrincipalPermission** object
- Performing role checks using the **IsInRole** method
- Performing role checks for custom authentication

Performing Declarative Demands Using the PrincipalPermissionAttribute

You can place demands at the class level, or at the member level on individual methods, properties, or events. If you place a declarative demand at both the class and member level, the declarative demand on the member overrides (or replaces) the demand at the class level.

The following code example shows a declarative demand for the **PrincipalPermission** object.

```
// Declarative example.
[PrincipalPermissionAttribute( SecurityAction.Demand, Role="Teller" )]
void SomeTellerOnlyMethod()
{
}
```

Performing Imperative Demands Using the PrincipalPermission Object

You can perform imperative demands by programmatically calling the **Demand** method of the **PrincipalPermission** object, as shown in the following code example.

```
// Programmatic example.
public SomeMethod()
{
    PrincipalPermission permCheck = new PrincipalPermission( null, "Teller" );
    permCheck.Demand();
    // Only Tellers can execute the following code.
    // Non members of the Teller role result in a security exception.
    . . .
}
```

One advantage of calling the method programmatically is that you can determine if the principal is in more than one role. The .NET Framework does not allow you to do this declaratively. The following code example shows how to perform the check.

```
// Using PrincipalPermission.
PrincipalPermission permCheckTellers = new PrincipalPermission( null, "Teller" );
permCheckTellers.Demand();
PrincipalPermission permCheckMgr = new PrincipalPermission( null, "Manager" );
permCheckMgr.Demand();
```

Performing Role Checks Using the IsInRole Method

You may choose to access the values of the principal object directly and perform checks without a **PrincipalPermission** object. In this case, you can read the values of the current thread's principal or use the **IsInRole** method to perform authorization, as shown in the following code example.

```
// Using IsInRole.
if ( Thread.CurrentPrincipal.IsInRole( "Teller" ) &&
     Thread.CurrentPrincipal.IsInRole( "Manager" ) )
{
    // Perform privileged operation.
}
```

Performing Role Checks for Custom Authentication

If your application is not Windows-based, you can programmatically populate a **GenericPrincipal** object with a set of roles obtained from a custom authentication data store such as a SQL Server database, as shown in the following code example.

```
GenericIdentity userIdentity = new GenericIdentity( "Bob" );
// Typically role names would be retrieved from a custom data store.
string[] roles = new String[]{ "Manager", "Teller" };
GenericPrincipal userPrincipal = new GenericPrincipal( userIdentity, roles );
if ( userPrincipal.IsInRole( "Teller" ) )
{
    // Perform privileged operation.
}
```

Authorization Guidelines

Authorization is critical to control user access to application functionality and resources accessed. Improper or weak authorization leads to information disclosure and data tampering. Consider the following authorization guidelines:

- **Use multiple gatekeepers where possible to enforce authorization checks when accessing resources or performing operations**. Using client checks combined with checks on the server provides defense in depth to prevent an attack from a malicious user who manages to bypass one of the gatekeepers. Common gatekeepers on the server include IIS Web permissions, NTFS file system permissions, Web service file authorization (which applies only with Windows authentication), and principal permission demands.

- **Authorize access to system resources using the security context of the user.** You can use role-based authorization to authorize access based on user identity and role membership. Integrated Windows authentication with Windows ACLs on the secured resources (such as files or the registry) determines whether the caller is allowed to access the resource. For assemblies, you can authorize calling code based on evidence, such as an assembly's strong name or location.

- **Ensure that roles are defined with enough granularity to adequately separate privileges.** Avoid granting elevated privileges just to satisfy the requirements of certain users; instead, consider adding new roles to meet those requirements.

- **Use declarative demands rather than imperative demands where possible.** Declarative demands provide or deny access to all of the method's functionality. They also work much better with security tools and help with security audits, because tools are able to access these demands by examining the application.

- **If you need to determine if the principal is in more than one role, consider imperative checks using IsInRole method.** The .NET Framework version 1.1 does not allow **AND** checks to be performed declaratively; however, they can be performed programmatically inside the method as shown in the following code example.

```
// Checking for multiple roles.
if ( Thread.CurrentPrincipal.IsInRole( "Teller" ) &&
     Thread.CurrentPrincipal.IsInRole( "Manager" ) )
{
    // Perform privileged operation.
}
```

- **Use code access security to authorize calling code access to privileged resources or operations, based on evidence, such as an assembly's strong name or location.** For more information, see "Code Access Security" later in this chapter.

Authorizing Functionality When the Client Is Offline

When users are connected to the network, they can be authorized directly against a network authorization store, but when they are not, they may still need to be authorized.

Any form of authorization is only as strong as the authentication mechanism used. If you allow anonymous authentication, you should be particularly careful about what functionality you allow users to access and generally should not authorize users to access system resources.

If you are authenticating users to use an application, you can let Windows act as the sole gatekeeper to determine which resources are available for the logged-on user profile. In this case, the user is often allowed to access local system resources.

You may choose to create different versions of the same application for different roles. When the user is connected to the network, he or she is allowed to install only the version of the application tailored to his or her role. Then, when the user runs the application offline, the correct functionality is automatically provided without the application being connected.

The Authorization and Profile Application Block

Microsoft offers an application block that provides infrastructure to simplify the inclusion of authorization functionality into your application.

The Authorization and Profile Application Block provides an infrastructure for role-based authorization and access to profile information. The block allows you to:

- Authorize a user of an application or system.
- Use multiple authorization storage providers.
- Plug in business rules for action validation.
- Map multiple identities to a single user, extending the idea of an identity to include authentication methods.
- Access profile information that can be stored in multiple profile stores.

For more information, see *Authorization and Profile Application Block* at *http://msdn.microsoft.com/library/default.asp?url=/library/en-us/dnpag/html/authpro.asp*.

Input Validation

Applications with poor input validation can be compromised by malicious input by an attacker. Validating user input is one of the first lines of defense for your application. Consider the following input validation guidelines for your smart client application:

- Ensure that your smart client application validates all input before processing or passing it to downstream resources and assemblies.
- Perform thorough validation of user input data if you are passing it to an unmanaged API. Doing so helps to prevent buffer overflows. You should limit user input of data that is passed to unmanaged APIs.
- Always validate data obtained from all external sources, such as Web sites and Web services.
- Never rely on client-side validation of data that is passed to your Web service or Web application. Validate data on the client and then validate it again on the server to prevent malicious input that bypasses client-side validation.

- Never allow users to enter SQL queries directly. Always provide prepackaged or parameterized queries that are thoroughly reviewed for security problems. Allowing users to enter SQL queries directly introduces the possibility of SQL injection attacks.

- Constrain and validate user input for known correct values or patterns, rather than for incorrect input. It is easier to check for a finite list of known values than to check for an infinite list of unknown malicious input types. You can either reject the bad input or sanitize it (that is, strip out potentially unsafe characters) before acting on it.

- Constrain input by validating it for type, length, format, and range. One way to do this is use to regular expressions (available from the **System.Text.RegularExpressions** namespace) to validate user input.

- Reject unknown bad data and then sanitize input. If your application needs to accept some user input in free form (for example, comments in a text box), you can sanitize the input as shown in the following example.

```
private string SanitizeInput( string input )
{
    // Example list of characters to remove from input.
    Regex badCharReplace = new Regex( @"([<>""'%;()&])" );
    string goodChars = badCharReplace.Replace( input, "" );
    return goodChars;
}
```

- Consider centralizing your validation routines to reduce development effort and aid future maintenance.

For more information, see "Input Validation" in "Chapter 4 — Design Guidelines for Secure Web Applications" of *Improving Web Application Security: Threats and Countermeasures* at *http://msdn.microsoft.com/library/default.asp?url=/library/en-us /dnnetsec/html/THCMCh04.asp.*

Handling Sensitive Data

If you are accustomed to designing Web applications, you understand the importance of securing stored data and data that is in transit. The data you store on a Web server is typically written to a physically secure location that is already well protected to prevent it from being attacked. In smart client applications, you also need to closely consider the data that resides on the client. If such data is sensitive, it is important that it is handled appropriately to ensure its security. To protect data in transit, you can secure the transport layer using SSL and securing the message contents using WS-Security or Message Queuing encryption tools.

Only data to which the user is authorized access should be made available to the client application. If the client application can be used by more than one person on a single computer, the data associated with each individual user should be considered sensitive data, and steps should be taken to ensure that only authorized users can access it.

Sensitive data includes any data that an attacker may find useful to access or modify, either because the information is confidential, or because it can help in an attack. Sensitive data may be data that the server provides to the client, but it can also include application configuration files, local databases, or registry information.

In general, you should try to ensure that sensitive data is not cached locally. However, in the case of a smart client application, you may need to cache this data (for example, to allow for occasionally connected operation by saving the data to a local store for later use).

Note: In some cases, sensitive data may be sent to disk as a result of paging from memory. Therefore, you should also consider data that is present in memory when determining what data needs to be encrypted.

Determining Which Data to Store on the Client

By definition, users, and therefore potential attackers, have physical access to clients. Given enough time, attackers are often able to obtain sufficient administrative access to access almost any data, so you should carefully consider what data should be persisted on the client. As a general rule, you should make authorization decisions on the server, so that the only data you pass from the server to the client is data that the user is allowed to access. In addition to improving performance, making authorization decisions on the server also ensures that the data is not available on the client for a potential attacker to access.

You should never store sensitive data in text-based files and should always encrypt the data so that it can be easily accessed only by authorized users. You should avoid using text-based configuration files to store sensitive security information, such as passwords or database connection strings. If this information must be stored locally, you should encrypt the information, store it in a file or registry key, and then restrict access to that object with a DACL. Any persisted data personal to the logged-on user must also be kept private and secure, particularly if the computer is shared between users.

In many cases, more data is stored on the client if the application needs to run offline. However, you should determine whether all of the data is required offline, or whether you want to restrict the user from performing certain actions when offline, so that you do not have to cache sensitive data locally.

In some cases, if data is confidential and can be entered by the user on demand, you may choose not to store it locally on the client at all and instead obtain it from the user as needed.

If your application needs to store sensitive data locally, you should usually avoid using removable storage (such as floppy disks, zip disks, or USB storage devices) or external portable storage to store sensitive data. However, user-specific data can be stored on removable media when you can be sure that the removable media is owned by that user (for example, by using a certificate or a smart card). Thus, user-specific data can be kept in a secure location that travels with the user, so that roaming users can access the application and their data without leaving that data on the local computer.

Note: As you consider which sensitive data to store on the client, you should ensure that by storing information about your employees or customers, you are not violating privacy regulations. These laws differ from country to country, so you should familiarize yourself with privacy regulations in the countries where your application is used.

Techniques for Protecting Sensitive Data

For data that you need to store at the client, there are a number of additional measures you can take to prevent unauthorized access. These include the following:

- Ensure that only authorized users can access data.
- Consider using EFS to encrypt files.
- Consider using DPAPI to avoid key management issues.
- Consider storing hash values instead of plain text.
- Consider isolated storage for partially trusted applications.
- Secure your private keys.

Ensure that Only Authorized Users can Access Data

Your data often needs to be protected to help make sure that only authorized users can access it. Depending on the nature of your application and how transient the data is, you may choose to use resource-based security or role-based security to protect your data. For more information, see "Authorization Guidelines" earlier in this chapter.

Consider Using EFS to Encrypt Files

One option for ensuring that files are held securely on smart clients is to use the Encrypting File System (EFS) to encrypt sensitive data files. This solution is not particularly scalable; however, it can be useful for specific files, and it may be useful for situations where you are caching data locally on the client (for example, to enable occasionally connected smart clients).

Consider Using DPAPI to Avoid Key Management Issues

Windows 2000 and later versions of the Windows operating system provide the Win32® Data Protection API (DPAPI) for encrypting and decrypting data. It is part of the Cryptography API (Crypto API) and is implemented in crypt32.dll. It consists of two methods, **CryptProtectData** and **CryptUnprotectData**.

DPAPI is particularly useful because it can eliminate the key management problem exposed to applications that use cryptography. While encryption ensures that the data is secure, you must take additional steps to ensure the security of the key. To derive the encryption key, DPAPI uses the password of the user account associated with the code that calls the DPAPI functions. As a result, the operating system (and not the application) manages the key.

DPAPI can work with either the machine store or user store. The user store is automatically loaded based on the logged-on user profile. Your client applications will mostly use DPAPI with the user store, unless there is need to store secrets common across all users who can log on to the computer.

The keys that DPAPI uses to encrypt and decrypt sensitive data are specific to a computer. A different key is generated for each computer, which prevents one server from being able to access data encrypted by another.

The unmanaged DPAPI requires assemblies to have full trust. Applications that have fully trusted and partially trusted assemblies can isolate code with high privileges and enable it to be called from partially trusted code. For more information, see "How To Create a Custom Encryption Permission" at *http://msdn.microsoft.com/library /default.asp?url=/library/en-us/secmod/html/secmod115.asp*.

Consider Storing Hash Values Instead of Plain Text

Sometimes data is stored so that it can be used to validate user input (for example, a user name and password combination). In such cases, rather than storing the data itself in plain text, you can store a cryptographic hash of the data. Then when the user input is made, that data can also be hashed, and the two hashes can be compared. Storing the hash reduces the risk of the secret being discovered because it is computationally impossible to deduce the original data from its hash, or to generate an identical hash from other data.

Consider Isolated Storage for Partially Trusted Applications

Isolated storage allows your application to save data to a unique data compartment that is associated with some aspect of the code's identity, such as its Web site, publisher, or signature. The data compartment is an abstraction, not a specific storage location; it consists of one or more isolated storage files, called stores, which contain the actual directory locations where data is stored.

Isolated storage can be particularly useful for partially trusted applications that need to store state data specific to particular users and assemblies. Partially trusted applications do not have direct access to the file system to persist state unless they have explicitly been granted permission to do so through a security policy change.

Data stored in isolated storage is isolated and protected from other partially trusted applications, but it is not protected from fully trusted code or from other users who have access to the client computer. To secure data in these scenarios, you should employ data encryption and file system security through the use of DACLs. For more information, see "Introduction to Isolated Storage" in the *.NET Framework Developer's Guide* at *http://msdn.microsoft.com/library/default.asp?url=/library/en-us/cpguide/html /cpconIntroductionToIsolatedStorage.asp*.

Protect Private Keys

Unprotected private keys are susceptible to a wide range of attacks by malicious users or malicious code. Private keys used to sign assemblies should not be left in insecure locations such as developers' computers or openly shared environments. Stolen private keys can be used by an attacker to sign malicious code with your strong name. You should strongly consider securing your private keys with a central security authority designated for this purpose within your organization. You can also keep your private keys on a physically secure, isolated computer, transferring the keys where necessary using portable media.

For more information about storing secrets effectively, see *Writing Secure Code, Second Edition*, by Michael Howard and David LeBlanc.

Code Access Security

Code access security is .NET Framework technology that applies authentication and authorization principles to code instead of users. Code access security can be a powerful mechanism for ensuring that only the code that you intended to run is run by the user.

All managed code is subject to code access security. When an assembly is loaded, it is granted a set of code access permissions that determine what resources it can access and what types of privileged operations it can perform. The .NET Framework security system uses evidence to authenticate (identify) code in order to grant these permissions.

Note: An assembly is the unit of configuration and trust for code access security. All code in the same assembly receives the same permissions and is therefore equally trusted.

Code access security consists of the following elements:

- **Permissions**. Permissions represent the rights for code to access a secured resource or perform a privileged operation. The Microsoft .NET Framework provides *code access permissions* and *code identity permissions*. Code access permissions encapsulate the ability to access a particular resource or perform a particular privileged operation. For example, the **FileIOPermission** is required before the application can perform any file I/O operations. Code identity permissions are used to restrict access to code, based on an aspect of the calling code's identity, such as its strong name.

- **Permission sets**. The .NET Framework defines a number of permission sets, which represent a group of permissions commonly assigned as a whole. For example, the .NET Framework defines the **FullTrust** permission set, which assigns all permissions to fully trusted code, and the **LocalIntranet** permission set, which assigns a very limited number of permissions.

- **Evidence**. Evidence is used by the .NET Framework security system to identify assemblies. Code access security policy uses evidence to help grant the right permissions to the right assembly. Evidence may be location-related (for example, URL, site, application directory, or zone) or author-related (for example, strong name, publisher, or hash).

- **Policy**. Code access security policy is configured by administrators and determines the permissions granted to assemblies. Policy can be established at the enterprise, machine, user, and application domain levels. Each policy is defined in an XML configuration file.

- **Code groups**. Each policy file contains a hierarchical collection of code groups. Code groups are used to assign permissions to assemblies. A code group consists of a membership condition (based on evidence) and a permission set. The .NET Framework defines a number of default code groups, such as the Internet, Local Intranet, Restricted, and Trusted zones.

For more detailed information about code access security, see the following chapters of *Improving Web Application Security: Threats and countermeasures*: "Chapter 7 — Building Secure Assemblies" at *http://msdn.microsoft.com/library/default.asp?url=/library /en-us/dnnetsec/html/THCMCh07.asp* and "Chapter 8 — Code Access Security in Practice" at *http://msdn.microsoft.com/library/default.asp?url=/library/en-us/dnnetsec/html /THCMCh08.asp*.

Code Access Security Permission Resolution

Code access security uses the steps outlined in Figure 5.2 to determine which permissions are assigned to an assembly.

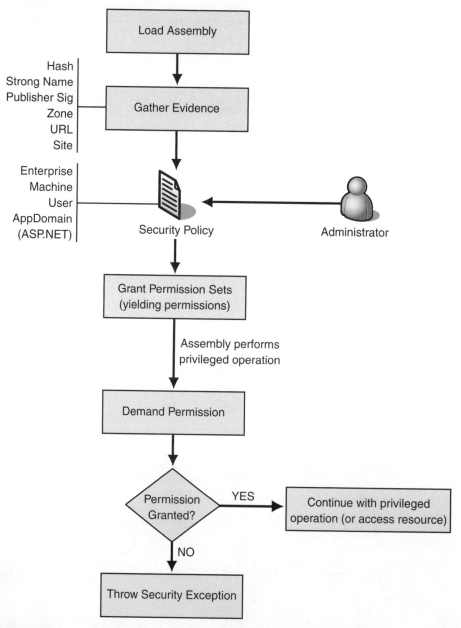

Figure 5.2

Determining which permissions are assigned to an assembly

The following steps outline the procedure in more detail:

1. An assembly is loaded, and evidence is gathered and presented to the host.
2. The evidence is evaluated against the security policy for the hosting environment.
3. The output of this evaluation is a set of permissions granted to the assembly. These permissions define what the assembly can and cannot do in this environment.
4. When the assembly asks to perform a privileged operation, the demands of that operation are compared with the permissions of the assembly. If the assembly has permission, the code is allowed to perform the operation; otherwise, a security exception is thrown.

Designing for Code Access Security

The permissions assigned to your code depend on the evidence associated with your code and the security policy in place on the client computer. To ensure the security of your application while maintaining its functionality, you need to carefully consider the permissions that your application requires, and the way in which these permissions are granted.

Applications that are granted all permissions (those applications defined in the FullTrust permission set) are known as fully trusted applications. Applications that are not granted all permissions are known as partially trusted applications.

In theory, it is generally preferable to design your applications to be partially trusted. However, smart client applications frequently need to perform a number of operations that partially trusted applications cannot perform by default. These operations include:

- Accessing servers other than the one from which the application was run or accessing servers that use a different protocol
- Accessing the local file system
- Accessing and interacting with local Microsoft Office applications
- Accessing and interacting with unmanaged code, such as COM objects

If your smart client is required to perform these kinds of operations, you should consider making it a fully trusted application or granting it the additional specific permissions it requires to operate properly.

Note: Applications deployed using no-touch deployment are automatically partially trusted by default. If your smart client needs to perform additional operations that cannot be performed by partially trusted applications, you either need to deploy a new security policy or use an alternative method to deploy the application.

Designing and building partially trusted applications can be challenging, but carefully considering and restricting the permissions granted to your application helps ensure that it cannot perform inappropriate actions or access resources that are not explicitly required.

All code must be granted permission to run before it can be run, but code that accesses secured resources or performs other security-sensitive operations (such as calling unmanaged code or accessing the local file system) must be granted additional permissions by the .NET Framework to be able to function. Such code is referred to as privileged code. Conversely, nonprivileged code does not require access to sensitive resources and requires only permission to run. When you design and build your application and its assemblies, you should identify and document privileged and nonprivileged code. Doing so helps you determine the permissions that your code requires.

You should also carefully examine which evidence is used by the .NET Framework to assign permissions to your code. Evidence based on the location of the application (for example, a file share or Web server) should be considered only if the central location is secure. Similarly, applications whose evidence is based on a common key used to sign all code (for example, by an organization's IT department) should be used only when the key is secure. However, it is generally more secure to rely on strong name evidence rather than any location-based evidence such as a Web server address.

Designing Partially Trusted Applications

Use the following guidelines when you design partially trusted applications:

- Know your application deployment scenarios.
- Avoid permissions demands that raise exceptions.
- Use the Demand/Assert pattern for partially trusted callers.
- Consider using strong names for your assemblies.
- Avoid giving full trust to restricted zones.

Know Your Application Deployment Scenarios

You should have a clear understanding of your application deployment scenarios during design, because the location to which your application is deployed has a significant effect on the permissions that the application is granted by default. Application functionalities such as displaying a dialog box (for example, using a **SaveFileDialog**) or accessing system resources may be restricted based on the deployment location of the application.

In particular, the permissions granted to your application depend on the zone in which it is located (for example, the Internet zone, Local Intranet zone, or Trusted zone). The user has some control over the application's membership in the Trusted zone, but you should not rely on the user to place your application in this zone to ensure correct functionality. You should design your application to fail gracefully if insufficient permissions are granted to it at run time.

If a user attempts to perform an action and the application does not have sufficient permissions to perform the action, the attempt may result in a failed permission demand, which in turn raises a security exception. Your application needs to handle these exceptions or it will fail. You should ensure that such failures are handled gracefully, and you should give the user enough information to address the problem without revealing inappropriate or sensitive security-related information.

Note: Applications deployed using the ClickOnce deployment features of the .NET Framework version 2.0 will be granted specific permissions according to their deployment manifest. The granted permissions will be fixed when the application is deployed, and the placement of the application's location in the Trusted zone will not affect the permissions that are granted.

Avoid Permission Demands that Raise Exceptions

Determine the permission required for each of your application functionalities to run properly without raising exceptions. Consider the following:

● **Design a workaround to avoid the permission demand that can cause exceptions**. For example, for intranet-based applications, instead of having the application automatically open and read a file from the hard disk, you can use **OpenFileDialog** to display a dialog box that instructs the user to select the file.

● **Check permissions to gracefully deal with exceptions (specifically, SecurityException)**. In your code, you can create an instance of a permission class specific to the resource that you are trying to access and check for necessary permissions before accessing the resource. For example, you can use the **FileDialogPermission** class and the **SecurityManager.IsGranted** static method to check for permissions when you have to display a dialog box using **OpenFileDialog** or **SaveFileDialog**, as follows.

```
FileDialogPermission fileDialogPermission = new
            FileDialogPermission( FileDialogPermissionAccess.Save );
if ( !SecurityManager.IsGranted( fileDialogPermission ) )
{
    // Not allowed to save file.
}
```

Note: IsGranted does not guarantee that an operation will succeed because it does not traverse the stack to determine whether all upstream code has the required permissions.

- Consider prototyping and testing your application scenario for various deployment zones:
  - If your application is designed to run from a file share, you can simulate this scenario by addressing the application as a network share (for example, \\MachineName\c$\YourAppPath\YourApp.exe) and running it from your hard disk.
  - If your application is designed to run from the Web Internet zone, you can use the IP address of your computer (for example, \\<MachineIPaddress\c$ \YourAppPath\YourApp.exe) to simulate this scenario.

Use the Demand/Assert Pattern for Partially Trusted Callers

The **Demand/Assert** pattern is used in fully trusted assemblies to allow access to privileged operations when called by partially trusted callers. This pattern is useful when a partially trusted caller needs to perform privileged operations in secure manner but does not have the necessary privileges. By using **Assert**, you vouch for the trustworthiness of your code's callers.

Note: The **Demand/Assert** pattern should be used only when you fully understand the security risks that its use can introduce. Asserting permissions turns off the normal .NET Framework permission checks, which check all of the calling code on the stack. Turning off this mechanism may introduce a serious security vulnerability into your code and should only be attempted when you fully understand its implications and have exhausted all other possible solutions.

In this pattern, the **Demand** calls occur before the **Assert** calls. The **Demand** checks to see if the caller has the permission, and then the **Assert** turns off the stack walk for the particular permission so that callers are not checked by the common language runtime to see they if have appropriate permissions.

For a partially trusted caller to successfully call a fully trusted assembly method, you can demand appropriate permissions to ensure that the partially trusted caller does not harm the system, and then assert the particular permission to perform the high privilege operation.

You should call **Assert** in your fully trusted assembly prior to making the privileged operation and call **RevertAssert** afterward to ensure that subsequent code in your method calls does not inadvertently succeed because the **Assert** is still in effect. You should place this code in a private function so that the **Assert** is removed from the stack automatically (using a **RevertAssert** call) after the method returns. It is important to make this method private so that an attacker cannot invoke the method using external code.

Consider the following example.

```
Private void PrivilegedOperation()
{
    // Demand for permission.
    new FileIOPermission( PermissionState.Unrestricted ).Demand();
    // Assert to allow caller with insufficient permissions.
    new FileIOPermission( PermissionState.Unrestricted ).Assert();
    // Perform your privileged operation.
}
```

By default, a fully trusted assembly does not allow calls from partially trusted applications or assemblies; such calls raise a security exception. To avoid these exceptions, you can add **AllowPartiallyTrustedCallersAttribute** (APTCA) to the AssemblyInfo.cs file generated by Visual Studio .NET as follows.

```
[assembly: AllowPartiallyTrustedCallersAttribute()]
```

Note: Code that uses APTCA should be reviewed to ensure that it cannot be exploited by any partially trusted malicious code. For more information, see "APTCA" in "Chapter 8 — Code Access Security in Practice" of *Improving Web Application Security: Threats and Countermeasures* at *http://msdn.microsoft.com/library/default.asp?url=/library/en-us/dnnetsec/html/THCMCh08.asp*.

Consider Using Strong-Named Assemblies

You can increase the security of your assemblies by using strong names for them. You should consider signing all of the assemblies in your application with a strong name, and modify the security policy to trust this strong name. You can sign the assembly with a strong name key pair using the Sn.exe tool. To change the security policy manually, you can use the .NET Framework Configuration MMC snap-in or Caspol.exe, a command line tool (located at %SystemRoot%\Microsoft.NET \Framework\<version>\CasPol.exe).

Your process for signing assemblies with private keys should take into account the following:

● **Use delayed signing for development**. The build process to compile code can use delayed signing, using the public portion of the strong name key pair instead of the private key. To use delayed signing, the developer can add the following attributes to the Assembly.cs file for your project.

```
[assembly:AssemblyKeyFile("publickey.snk")]
[assembly:AssemblyDelaySign(true)]
```

- **Secure the generated private keys**. The following command line shows the use of the strong name tool (Sn.exe), which is provided with the .NET Framework SDK, to generate the key pair (Keypair.snk) directly to a removable storage device. (In the example, the F drive used is a USB drive.)

```
sn -k f:\keypair.snk
sn -p f:\keypair.snk f:\publickey.snk
```

The public key (Publickey.snk) is used for delayed signing by the developers. The key pair is stored in a secure location with highly restricted access.

- **Disable verification for testing**. To test an assembly that has been delay signed, you can register it on test computers by using Sn.exe. Table 5.1 lists the commonly used command-line variations.

Table 5.1: Commonly Used Command-Line Variations

Command	Description
sn -Vr assembly.dll	Disable verification for a specific assembly.
sn -Vr *,publickeytoken	Disable verification for all assemblies with a particular public key. The asterisk (*) registers all delayed signed assemblies by a key corresponding to the provided public key token for verification skipping.

- **Sign with the private key for release**. To complete the signing process, use the following command to sign with the private key.

```
sn -r assembly.dll f:\keypair.snk
```

Designated team members should then test and review the assembly, before signing it off for use in the organization.

For more information about delayed signing and the process explained in this section, see the following resources in *Improving Web Application Security: Threats and Countermeasures*:

- "Chapter 3 — Threat Modeling," at *http://msdn.microsoft.com/library/default.asp?url=/library/en-us/dnnetsec/html/THCMCh03.asp*.
- "Delay Signing" in "Chapter 7 — Building Secure Assemblies" at *http://msdn.microsoft.com/library/default.asp?url=/library/en-us/dnnetsec/html/THCMCh07.asp*.
- "Chapter 5 — Architecture and Design Review for Security" at *http://msdn.microsoft.com/library/default.asp?url=/library/en-us/dnnetsec/html/THCMCh05.asp*.
- "Chapter 21 — Code Review" at *http://msdn.microsoft.com/library/default.asp?url=/library/en-us/dnnetsec/html/THCMCh21.asp*.

See the article, "Strong Name Signing Using Smart Cards in Enterprise Software Production Environment" at *http://www.dotnetthis.com/Articles/SNandSmartCards.htm*.

Avoid Giving Full Trust to Restricted Zones

As a quick workaround to resolve the security issues with partially trusted applications, you might be tempted to give full trust to restricted zones such as the Internet or Local Intranet zone. Doing so allows any application to run without code access security checks on your local system, which becomes an issue if the application is from a malicious source. However, if deployment scenarios are considered during the design phase, you should not have to open up security to allow applications to run.

Designing Fully Trusted Applications

Because partially trusted applications may have very little access to system resources, your application may require more permissions than are assigned to it by default to operate properly. Applications that need to be able to perform tasks such as launching Office applications or Microsoft Internet Explorer, calling into legacy COM components, or writing to the file system need to run with permissions that enable these operations explicitly.

It can be tempting to assign your application as a fully trusted application so that it is assigned all possible permissions. However, it is more secure to design and deploy your application to request the minimum amount of permissions required for it to operate properly. If you do need to run your application as a fully trusted application, you should consider the following guidelines:

- Identify the types of resources your assembly needs to access and assess the potential threats that are likely to occur if the assembly is compromised.
- Identify the trust level of your target environment because code access security policy may constrain what your assembly is allowed to do.
- Reduce the attack surface by using the public access modifier only for classes and members that form part of the assembly's public interface. Wherever possible, restrict access to all other classes and members using private or protected access modifier.
- Use the **sealed** keyword to prevent inheritance of classes that are not designed as a base class as shown in the following code.

```
public sealed class NobodyDerivesFromMe
{...}
```

- Where possible, use declarative class level or method level attributes to restrict access to members of the specified Windows group as shown in the following code.

```
[PrincipalPermission(SecurityAction.Demand,Role=@"DomainName\WindowsGroup")]
public sealed class Orders()
{...}
```

- Establish a secure build process for delayed signing, testing, security reviews, and securing the private keys.

Summary

Smart client applications are distributed applications. Therefore, to manage security effectively for them, you need to consider security at the server, the client, and the network connection between the two. Specific smart client considerations include designing secure authentication, authorization, data validation, and securing sensitive data. You should also examine how to use code access security, to manage security at code level rather than user level.

6

Using Multiple Threads

A thread is a basic unit of execution. A single thread executes a series of application instructions, following a single path of logic through the application. All applications have at least one thread, but you can design your applications so that they use multiple threads, with each thread executing separate logic. By using multiple threads in your application, you can process lengthy or time-consuming tasks in the background. Even on a computer with a single processor, the use of multiple threads can significantly improve the responsiveness and usability of your application.

Developing your application to use multiple threads can be very complicated, particularly if you do not carefully consider locking and synchronization issues. As you develop your smart client application, you need to carefully evaluate where and how multiple threads should be used so that you can gain maximum advantage without creating applications that are unnecessarily complex and difficult to debug.

This chapter examines some of the concepts that are most important for developing multithreaded smart client applications. It looks at some of the recommended uses for multiple threads in a smart client application, and it describes how to implement these capabilities.

Multithreading in the .NET Framework

All .NET Framework applications are created with a single thread, which is used to execute the application. In smart client applications, this thread creates and manages the user interface (UI) and is called the UI thread.

You can use the UI thread for all processing, including Web service calls, remote object calls, and calls into a database. However, using the UI thread in this way is generally not a good idea. In most cases, you will be unable to predict how long a call to a Web service, remote object, or database will take, and you may cause the UI to freeze while the UI thread waits for a response.

Creating additional threads enables your application to perform additional processing without using the UI thread. You can use multiple threads to prevent the UI from freezing while the application makes a Web service call, or to perform certain local tasks in parallel to increase the overall efficiency of your application. In most cases, you should strongly consider performing any tasks not related to the UI on a separate thread.

Choosing Between Synchronous and Asynchronous Calls

Applications can make both synchronous and asynchronous calls. A *synchronous* call waits for a response or return value before proceeding. A call is said to be *blocked* if it is not allowed to proceed.

An *asynchronous*, or *nonblocking* call, does not wait for a response. Asynchronous calls are carried out by using a separate thread. The original thread initiates the asynchronous call, which uses another thread to carry out the request while the original thread continues processing.

With smart client applications, it is important to minimize synchronous calls from the UI thread. As you design your smart client application, you should consider each call your application will make and determine whether a synchronous call may negatively affect the application's responsiveness and performance.

Use synchronous calls from the UI thread only when:

- Performing operations that manipulate the UI
- Performing small, well-defined operations that pose no risk of causing the UI to freeze

Use asynchronous calls from the UI thread when:

- Performing background operations that do not affect the UI
- Making calls into other systems or resources located on the network
- Performing operations that may take a long time to complete

Choosing Between Foreground and Background Threads

All threads in the .NET Framework are designated as foreground threads or background threads. The two have only one difference — background threads do not prevent a process from terminating. After all foreground threads belonging to a process have terminated, the common language runtime (CLR) ends the process, terminating any background threads that are still running.

By default, all threads generated by creating and starting a new **Thread** object are foreground threads, and all threads that enter the managed execution environment from unmanaged code are marked as background threads. However, you can modify whether a thread is a foreground or background thread by modifying the **Thread.IsBackground** property. A thread is designated as a background thread by setting **Thread.IsBackground** to **true**, and is designated a foreground thread by setting **Thread.IsBackground** to **false**.

Note: For more information about the **Thread** object, see "Using the Thread Class" later in this chapter.

In most applications, you will choose to set different threads as either foreground or background threads. Usually, you should set threads that passively listen for an activity as background threads, and set threads responsible for sending data as foreground threads so that the thread is not terminated before all the data is sent.

You should use background threads only when you are sure that there will be no adverse effects of the thread being unceremoniously terminated by the system. Use a foreground thread when the thread is performing sensitive or transactional operations that need to be completed, or when you need to control how the thread is shut down so that important resources can be released.

Handling Locking and Synchronization

Sometimes when you build applications, you create multiple threads that all need to use key resources, such as data or application components, at the same time. If you are not careful, one thread could make a change to a resource while another thread is working with it. The result may be that the resource is left in an indeterminate state and is rendered unusable. This is known as a *race condition*. Other adverse effects of using multiple threads without carefully considering shared resource usage include deadlocks, thread starvation, and thread affinity issues.

To prevent these effects when accessing a resource from two or more threads, you need to coordinate the threads that are trying to access the resource by using locking and synchronization techniques.

Managing thread access to shared resources using locking and synchronization is a complex task and should be avoided wherever possible by passing data between threads rather than providing shared access to a single instance.

If you can't eliminate resource sharing between threads, you should:

- Use the **lock** statement in Microsoft Visual C#® and the **SyncLock** statement in Microsoft® Visual Basic® .NET to create a critical section, but beware of making method calls from within a critical section to prevent deadlocks.
- Use the **Synchronized** method to obtain thread-safe .NET collections.
- Use the **ThreadStatic** attribute to create per-thread members.
- Use a double-check lock or the **Interlocked.CompareExchange** method to prevent unnecessary locking.
- Ensure that static state is thread safe.

For more information about locking and synchronization techniques, see "Threading Design Guidelines" in *.NET Framework General Reference* at *http://msdn.microsoft.com /library/default.asp?url=/library/en-us/cpgenref/html/cpconthreadingdesignguidelines.asp*.

Using Timers

In some situations, you may not need to use a separate thread. If your application needs to perform simple, UI-related operations periodically, you should consider using a process timer. Process timers are sometimes used in smart client applications to:

- Perform operations at regularly scheduled times.
- Maintain consistent animation speeds (regardless of processor speed) when working with graphics.
- Monitor servers and other applications to confirm that they are online and running.

The .NET Framework provides three process timers:

- **System.Window.Forms.Timer**
- **System.Timers.Timer**
- **System.Threading.Timer**

System.Window.Forms.Timer is useful if you want to raise events in a Windows Forms application. It is specifically optimized to work with Windows Forms and must be used within a Windows Form. It is designed to work in a single-threaded environment and operates synchronously on the UI thread. This means that this timer will never preempt the execution of application code (assuming that you do not call **Application.DoEvents**) and is safe to interact with the UI.

System.Timers.Timer is designed and optimized for use in multithreaded environments. Unlike **System.Window.Forms.Timer**, this timer calls your event handler on a worker thread obtained from the CLR thread pool. You should ensure that the event handler does not interact with the UI in this case. **System.Timers.Timer** exposes a **SynchronizingObject** property that can mimic behavior from **System.Windows.Forms.Timer**, but unless you need more precise control over the timing of the events, you should use **System.Windows.Forms.Timer** instead.

System.Threading.Timer is a simple, lightweight server-side timer. It is not inherently thread safe and it is more cumbersome to use than other timers. This timer is generally not suitable for Windows Forms environments.

Table 6.1 lists the various properties of each timer.

Table 6.1: Process Timer Properties

Property	System.Windows.Forms	System.Timers	System.Threading
Timer event runs on what thread?	UI thread	UI or worker thread	Worker thread
Instances are thread safe?	No	Yes	No
Requires Windows Forms?	Yes	No	No
Initial timer event can be scheduled?	No	No	Yes

When to Use Multiple Threads

Multithreading can be used in many common situations to significantly improve the responsiveness and usability of your application.

You should strongly consider using multiple threads to:

- Communicate over a network, for example to a Web server, database, or remote object.
- Perform time-consuming local operations that would cause the UI to freeze.
- Distinguish tasks of varying priority.
- Improve the performance of application startup and initialization.

It is useful to examine these uses in more detail.

Communicating Over a Network

Smart-clients may communicate over a network in a number of ways, including:

- Remote object calls, such as DCOM, RPC or .NET remoting
- Message-based communications, such as Web service calls and HTTP requests
- Distributed transactions

Many factors determine how fast a network service responds to an application making a request, including the nature of the request, network latency, reliability and bandwidth of a connection, and how busy the service or services are.

This unpredictability can cause problems with the responsiveness of single-threaded applications, and multithreading is often a good solution. You should create a separate thread to the UI thread for all communication over a network, and then pass the data back to the UI thread when a response is received.

It is not always necessary to create separate threads for network communication. If your application communicates over the network asynchronously, for example using Microsoft Windows Message Queuing (also known as MSMQ), it does not wait for a response before continuing. However, even in this case, you should still use a separate thread to listen for and process the response when it arrives.

Performing Local Operations

Even in situations where processing occurs locally, some operations may take enough time to negatively affect the responsiveness of your application. Such operations include:

- Image rendering
- Data manipulation
- Data sorting
- Searching

You should not perform operations such as these on the UI thread because doing so causes performance problems in your application. Instead, you should use an additional thread to perform these operations asynchronously and prevent the UI thread from blocking.

In many cases, you should also design the application so that it reports the progress and success or failure of ongoing background operations. You may also consider allowing the user to cancel background operations to improve usability.

Distinguishing Tasks of Varying Priority

Not all of the tasks your application has to perform will be of the same priority. Some tasks will be time critical, and others will not. In other cases, you may find that one thread is dependent on the results of processing on another thread.

You should create threads of different priorities to reflect the priorities of the tasks they are performing. For example, you should use a high-priority thread to manage time-critical tasks, and a low-priority thread to perform passive tasks or tasks that are not time-sensitive.

Application Startup

Your application often has to perform a number of operations when it first runs. For example, it may need to initialize its state, retrieve or update data, and open connections to local resources. You should consider using a separate thread to initialize your application, allowing the user to start using the application as soon as possible. Using a separate thread for initialization increases your application's responsiveness and usability.

If you do perform initialization on a separate thread, you should prevent the user from initiating operations that depend on initialization being completed, by updating the UI menu and toolbar button state after initialization is complete. You should also provide clear feedback that notifies users of the initialization progress.

Creating and Using Threads

There are several ways that you can create and use background threads in the .NET Framework. You can use the **ThreadPool** class to access the pool of threads managed by the .NET Framework for a given process, or you can use the **Thread** class to explicitly create and manage a thread. Alternatively, you can use delegate objects or a Web service proxy to cause specific processing to occur on a non-UI thread. This section examines each of these different methods in turn and makes recommendations about when each should be used.

Using the ThreadPool Class

By now you probably realize that many of your applications would benefit from multithreading. However, thread management is not just a question of creating a new thread each time you want to perform a different task. Having too many threads can cause an application to use an unnecessary number of system resources, particularly if you have a large number of short-running operations, all of which are running on separate threads. Also, managing a large number of threads explicitly can be very complex.

Thread pooling solves these problems by providing your application with a pool of worker threads that are managed by the system, allowing you to concentrate on application tasks rather than thread management.

Threads can be added to the thread pool as required by the application. When the CLR initially starts, the thread pool contains no additional threads. However, as your application requests threads, they are dynamically created and stored in the pool. If threads are not used for some time, they can be disposed of, so the thread pool shrinks and grows according to the demands of the application.

Note: One thread pool is created per process, so if you run several application domains within the same process, an error in one application domain can affect the rest within the same process because they use the same thread pool.

A thread pool consists of two types of threads:

- **Worker threads**. The worker threads are part of the standard system pool. They are standard threads managed by the .NET Framework, and most functions are executed on them.

- **Completion port threads**. This kind of thread is used for asynchronous I/O operations, using the IOCompletionPorts API.

  Note: If the application is trying to perform I/O operations with a computer that does not have IOCompletionPorts functionality, it will revert to using worker threads.

The thread pool contains a default of 25 threads per computer processor. If all 25 threads are being used, additional requests queue until a thread becomes available. Each thread uses the default stack size and runs at the default priority.

The following code example shows the use of a thread pool.

```
private void ThreadPoolExample()
{
    WaitCallback callback = new WaitCallback( ThreadProc );
    ThreadPool.QueueUserWorkItem( callback );
}
```

In the preceding code, you first create a delegate to reference the code you want executed on a worker thread. The .NET Framework defines the **WaitCallback** delegate, which references a method that takes a single object parameter and returns no values. The following method implements the code you want executed.

```
private void ThreadProc( Object stateInfo )
{
    // Do something on worker thread.
}
```

You can pass a single object argument to the **ThreadProc** method by specifying it as the second parameter in the **QueueUserWorkItem** method call. In the preceding example, no arguments are passed to the **ThreadProc** method, so the **stateInfo** parameter will be null.

Use the **ThreadPool** class when:

- You have a large number of small and independent tasks that are to be performed in the background.
- You do not need to have fine control over the thread used to perform a task.

Using the Thread Class

You can explicitly manage threads by using the **Thread** class. This includes threads created by the CLR and those created outside the CLR that enter the managed environment to execute code. The CLR monitors all of the threads in its process that have ever executed code within the .NET Framework and uses an instance of the **Thread** class to manage them.

Whenever you can, you should create threads using the **ThreadPool** class. However, there are several situations where you will need to create and manage your own threads instead of using the **ThreadPool** class.

Use a **Thread** object when:

- You need a task to have a particular priority.
- You have a task that might run a long time (and therefore might block other tasks).
- You need to ensure that particular assemblies can be accessed by only one thread.
- You need to have a stable identity associated with the thread.

The **Thread** object contains a number of properties and methods that help you control threads. You can set the priority of thread, query the current thread state, abort threads, temporarily block threads, and perform many other thread management tasks.

The following code example demonstrates the use of the **Thread** object to create and start a thread.

```
static void Main()
{
    System.Threading.Thread workerThread =
        new System.Threading.Thread( SomeDelegate );
    workerThread.Start();
}
public static void SomeDelegate () { Console.WriteLine( "Do some work." ); }
```

In this example, SomeDelegate is a **ThreadStart** delegate — a reference to the code that will be executed on the new thread. **Thread.Start** submits a request to the operating system to start the thread.

If you instantiate a new thread this way, you cannot pass any arguments to the **ThreadStart** delegate. If you need to pass an argument to a method to be executed on another thread, you should create a custom delegate with the required method signature and invoke it asynchronously.

For more information about custom delegates, see "Using Delegates" later in this chapter.

If you need to receive updates or results from a separate thread, you can use a callback method — a delegate that references code to be called after the thread finishes its work — that allows threads to interact with the UI. For more information, see "Using Tasks to Handle Interactions Between the UI Thread and Other Threads" later in this chapter.

Using Delegates

A delegate is a reference (or a pointer) to a method. When you define a delegate, you specify the exact method signature that other methods must match if they want to represent the delegate. All delegates can be invoked both synchronously and asynchronously.

The following code example shows how to declare a delegate. This example shows a long-running calculation implemented as a method in a class.

```
delegate string LongCalculationDelegate( int count );
```

If the .NET Framework encounters a delegate declaration like the previous one, it implicitly declares a hidden class derived from the **MultiCastDelegate** class, as shown in the following code example.

```
Class LongCalculationDelegate : MutlicastDelegate
{
    public string Invoke( count );
    public void BeginInvoke( int count, AsyncCallback callback,
        object asyncState );
    public string EndInvoke( IAsyncResult result );
}
```

The delegate type **LongCalculationDelegate** is used to reference a method that takes a single integer parameter and returns a string. The following code example instantiates a delegate of this type that references a specific method with the relevant signature.

```
LongCalculationDelegate longCalcDelegate =
            new LongCalculationDelegate( calculationMethod );
```

In the example, **calculationMethod** is the name of a method that implements the calculation you want performed on a separate thread.

You can invoke the method referenced by the delegate instance either synchronously or asynchronously. To invoke it synchronously, use the following code.

```
string result = longCalcDelegate( 10000 );
```

This code internally uses the **Invoke** method defined in the delegate type above. Because the **Invoke** method is a synchronous call, this method returns only after the invoked method returns. The return value is the result of the invoked method.

More frequently, to prevent the calling thread from blocking, you will choose to invoke the delegate asynchronously, using the **BeginInvoke** and **EndInvoke** methods. Asynchronous delegates use the thread pooling capabilities of the .NET Framework for thread management. The standard *Asynchronous Call* pattern implemented by the .NET Framework provides the **BeginInvoke** method to initiate the required operation on a thread, and it provides the **EndInvoke** method to allow the asynchronous operation to be completed and any resulting data to be passed back to the calling thread. After the background processing completes, you can invoke a callback method within which you can call **EndInvoke** to retrieve the result of the asynchronous operation.

When you call the **BeginInvoke** method, it does not wait for the call to complete; instead, it immediately returns an **IAsyncResult** object, which can be used to monitor the progress of the call. You can use the **WaitHandle** member of the **IAsyncResult** object to wait for the asynchronous call to complete or use the **IsComplete** member to poll for completion. If you call the **EndInvoke** method before the call completes, it will block and return only after the call completes. However, you should be careful not to use these techniques to wait for the call to complete, because they may block the UI thread. In general, the callback mechanism is the best way to be notified that the call has completed.

▶ **To execute a method referenced by a delegate asynchronously**

1. Define a delegate representing the long-running asynchronous operation, as shown in the following example.

    ```
    delegate string LongCalculationDelegate( int count );
    ```

2. Define a method matching the delegate signature. The following example method simulates a time-consuming operation by causing the thread to sleep for **count** milliseconds before returning.

    ```
    private string LongCalculation( int count )
    {
        Thread.Sleep( count );
        return count.ToString();
    }
    ```

3. Define a callback method that corresponds to the **AsyncCallback** delegate defined by the .NET Framework, as shown in the following example.

```
private void CallbackMethod( IAsyncResult ar )
{
    // Retrieve the invoking delegate.
    LongCalculationDelegate dlgt = (LongCalculationDelegate)ar.AsyncState;
    // Call EndInvoke to retrieve the results.
    string results = dlgt.EndInvoke(ar);
}
```

4. Create an instance of a delegate that references the method you want to call asynchronously and create an **AsyncCallback** delegate that references the callback method, as shown in the following code example.

```
LongCalculationDelegate longCalcDelegate =
        new LongCalculationDelegate( calculationMethod );
AsyncCallback callback = new AsyncCallback( CallbackMethod );
```

5. From your calling thread, initiate the asynchronous call by calling the **BeginInvoke** method on the delegate that references the code you want to execute asynchronously.

```
longCalcDelegate.BeginInvoke( count, callback, longCalcDelegate );
```

The method **LongCalculation** is called on the worker thread. When it completes, the method **CallbackMethod** is called, and the results of the calculation retrieved.

Note: The callback method is executed on a non-UI thread. To modify the UI, you need to use techniques to switch from this thread to the UI thread. For more information, see "Using Tasks to Handle Interactions Between the UI Thread and Other Threads" later in this chapter.

You can use a custom delegate to pass arbitrary parameters to a method to be executed on a separate thread (something you cannot do when you create threads directly using either the **Thread** object or a thread pool.)

Invoking delegates asynchronously is particularly useful when you need to invoke long-running operations in the application UI. If users perform an operation in the UI that is expected to take a long time to complete, you do not want the UI to freeze and not be able to refresh itself. Using an asynchronous delegate, you can return control to your main UI thread to perform other operations.

You should use a delegate to invoke a method asynchronously when:

- You need to pass arbitrary parameters to a method you want to execute asynchronously.
- You want to use the *Asynchronous Call* pattern provided by the .NET Framework.

Note: For more details about how to use **BeginInvoke** and **EndInvoke** to make asynchronous calls, see "Asynchronous Programming Overview" in the *.NET Framework Developer's Guide* at *http://msdn.microsoft.com/library/default.asp?url=/library/en-us/cpguide/html /cpovrasynchronousprogrammingoverview.asp*.

Calling Web Services Asynchronously

Applications often communicate with network resources using Web services. In general, you should not call a Web service synchronously from the UI thread, because response times to Web service calls vary widely, as do response times in all interactions over the network. Instead, you should call all Web services asynchronously from the client.

To see how to call Web services asynchronously, consider the following simple Web service, which sleeps for a period of time and then returns a string indicating that it has completed its operation.

```
[WebMethod]
public string ReturnMessageAfterDelay( int delay )
{
    System.Threading.Thread.Sleep(delay);
    return "Message Received";
}
```

When you reference a Web service in the Microsoft Visual Studio® .NET development system, it automatically generates a proxy. A proxy is a class that allows your Web services to be invoked asynchronously using the *Asynchronous Call* pattern implemented by the .NET Framework. If you examine the proxy that is generated, you will see the following three methods.

```
public string ReturnMessageAfterDelay( int delay )
{
    object[] results = this.Invoke( "ReturnMessageAfterDelay",
                              new object[] {delay} );
    return ((string)(results[0]));
}
public System.IAsyncResult BeginReturnMessageAfterDelay( int delay,
                      System.AsyncCallback callback, object asyncState )
{
    return this.BeginInvoke( "ReturnMessageAfterDelay",
                      new object[] {delay}, callback, asyncState );
}
public string EndReturnMessageAfterDelay( System.IAsyncResult asyncResult )
{
    object[] results = this.EndInvoke( asyncResult );
    return ((string)(results[0]));
}
```

The first method is the synchronous method for invoking the Web service. The second and third methods are asynchronous methods. You can call the Web service asynchronously as follows.

```
private void CallWebService()
{
    localhost.LongRunningService serviceProxy =
                    new localhost.LongRunningService();
    AsyncCallback callback = new AsyncCallback( Completed );
    serviceProxy.BeginReturnMessageAfterDelay( callback, serviceProxy, null );
}
```

This example is very similar to the asynchronous callback example using a custom delegate. You define an **AsyncCallback** object with a method that will be invoked when the Web service returns. You invoke the asynchronous Web service with a method that specifies the callback and the proxy itself, as shown in the following code example.

```
void Completed( IAsyncResult ar )
{
    localhost.LongRunningService serviceProxy =
        (localhost.LongRunningService)ar.AsyncState;
    string message = serviceProxy.EndReturnMessageAfterDelay( ar );
}
```

When the Web service completes, the completed callback method is called. You can then retrieve your asynchronous result by calling **EndReturnMessageAfterDelay** on the proxy.

Using Tasks to Handle Interaction Between the UI Thread and Other Threads

One of the most challenging aspects of designing multithreaded applications is handling the relationship between the UI thread and other threads. It is critical that the background threads you use in your application do not directly interact with the application UI. If a background thread tries to modify a control in the UI of your application, the control can be left in an unknown state. This can cause major problems in your application that are difficult to diagnose. For example, a dynamically generated bitmap may be unable to render while another thread is feeding it new data. Or, a component bound to a dataset may display conflicting information while the dataset is being refreshed.

To avoid these problems, you should never allow threads other than the UI thread to make changes to UI controls, or to data objects bound to the UI. You should always try and maintain a strict separation between the UI code and the background processing code.

Separating the UI thread from the other threads is good practice, but you still need to pass information back and forth between the threads. Your multithreaded application will typically need to be capable of the following:

- Obtaining the results from a background thread and updating the UI.
- Reporting progress to the UI as a background thread performs its processing.
- Controlling the background thread from the UI, for example letting the user cancel the background processing.

An effective way to separate the UI code from the code that handles the background thread is to structure your application in terms of tasks, and to represent each task using an object that encapsulates all of the task details.

A task is a unit of work that the user expects to be able to carry out within the application. In the context of multithreading, the **Task** object encapsulates all of the threading details so that they are cleanly separated from the UI.

By using the *Task* pattern, you can simplify your code when using multiple threads. The *Task* pattern clearly separates thread management code from UI code. The UI uses properties and methods provided by the **Task** object to perform actions such as starting and stopping tasks, and to query them for status. The **Task** object can also provide a number of events, allowing status information to be passed back to the UI. These events should all be fired on the UI thread so that the UI does not need to be aware of the background thread.

You can simplify thread interactions substantially by using a **Task** object that is responsible for controlling and managing the background thread but fires events that can be consumed by the UI and guaranteed to be on the UI thread. **Task** objects can be reused in various parts of the application, or even in other applications.

Figure 6.1 illustrates the overall structure of the code when you use the *Task* pattern.

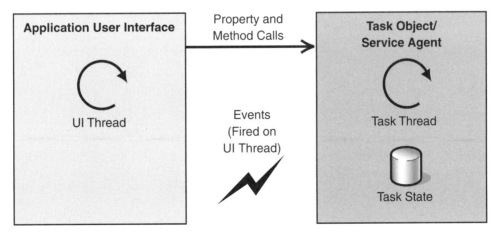

Figure 6.1
Code structure when using the Task pattern

Note: The *Task* pattern can be used to perform local background processing tasks on a separate thread or to interact with a remote service over the network asynchronously. In the latter case, the **Task** object is often called a service agent. A service agent can use the same pattern as the **Task** object and can support properties and events that make its interaction with the UI easier.

Because the **Task** object encapsulates the state of the task, you can use it to update the UI. To do so, you can have the **Task** object fire **PropertyChanged** events to the main UI thread whenever a change occurs. These events provide a standard, consistent way to communicate property value changes.

You can use tasks to inform the main UI thread of progress or other state changes. For example, when a task becomes available, you can set its enabled flag, which can be used to enable the corresponding menu item and toolbar buttons. Conversely, when a task becomes unavailable (for example, because it is in progress), you can set the enabled flag to false, which causes the event hander in the main UI thread to disable the correct menu items and toolbar buttons.

You can also use tasks to update data objects that are bound to the UI. You should ensure that any data objects that are data bound to UI controls are updated on the UI thread. For example, if you bind a **DataSet** object to the UI and retrieve updated information from a Web service, you can pass the new data to your UI code. The UI code then merges the new data into the bound **DataSet** on the UI thread.

You can use a **Task** object to implement background processing and threading control logic. Because the **Task** object encapsulates the necessary state and data, it can coordinate the work required to carry out the task on one or more threads and communicate changes and notifications to the application's UI as required. All required locking and synchronization can be implemented and encapsulated in the **Task** object, so that the UI thread does not have to deal with these issues.

Defining a Task Class

The following code example shows a class definition for a task that manages a long calculation.

Note: Although this example is simple, it can be easily extended to support complex background tasks that are integrated in the application's UI.

```
public class CalculationTask
{
    // Class Members...

    public CalculationTask();
    public void StartCalculation( int count );
    public void StopCalculation();

    private void FireStatusChangedEvent( CalculationStatus status );
    private void FireProgressChangedEvent( int progress );
    private string Calculate( int count );
    private void EndCalculate( IAsyncResult ar );
}
```

The **CalculationTask** class defines a default constructor and two public methods for starting and stopping the calculation. It also defines helper methods that help the **Task** object to fire events to the UI. The **Calculate** method implements the calculation logic and is run on a background thread. The **EndCalculate** method implements the callback method, which is called after the background calculation thread has completed.

The class members are as follows:

```
private CalculationStatus _calcState;

private delegate string CalculationDelegate( int count );

public delegate void CalculationStatusEventHandler(
            object sender, CalculationEventArgs e );

public delegate void CalculationProgressEventHandler(
            object sender, CalculationEventArgs e );

public event CalculationStatusEventHandler CalculationStatusChanged;
public event CalculationProgressEventHandler CalculationProgressChanged;
```

The **CalculationStatus** member is an enumeration that defines the three states that the calculation can be in at any one time.

```
public enum CalculationStatus
{
    NotCalculating,
    Calculating,
    CancelPending
}
```

The **Task** class provides two events: one to inform the UI about calculation status events, and the other to inform the UI about calculation progress. The delegate signatures are defined as well as the events themselves.

The two events are fired in the helper methods. These methods check the type of the target; if the target's type is derived from the **Control** class, they fire the events by using the **Invoke** method on the control class. Therefore, for UI event sinks, the event is guaranteed to be called on the UI thread. The following example shows the code for firing the event.

```
private void FireStatusChangedEvent( CalculationStatus status )
{
    if( CalculationStatusChanged != null )
    {
        CalculationEventArgs args = new CalculationEventArgs( status );
        if ( CalculationStatusChanged.Target is
                System.Windows.Forms.Control )
        {
            Control targetForm = CalculationStatusChanged.Target
                    as System.Windows.Forms.Control;
            targetForm.Invoke( CalculationStatusChanged,
                    new object[] { this, args } );
        }
        else
        {
            CalculationStatusChanged( this, args );
        }
    }
}
```

This code first checks to see if an event sink has been registered, and if it has been registered, it checks the type of the target. If the target's type is derived from the **Control** class, the event is fired using the **Invoke** method to ensure that it is processed on the UI thread. If the target's type is not derived from the **Control** class, the event is fired normally. Events are fired in the same way to report calculation progress to the UI in the **FireProgressChangedEvent** method, as shown in the following example.

```
private void FireProgressChangedEvent( int progress )
    {
        if( CalculationProgressChanged != null )
        {
            CalculationEventArgs args =
                new CalculationEventArgs( progress );
            if ( CalculationStatusChanged.Target is
                    System.Windows.Forms.Control )
            {
                Control targetForm = CalculationStatusChanged.Target
                        as System.Windows.Forms.Control;
                targetForm.Invoke( CalculationProgressChanged,
                        new object[] { this, args } );
            }
            else
            {
                CalculationProgressChanged( this, args );
            }
        }
    }
}
```

The **CalculationEventArgs** class defines the event arguments for both events and contains the calculation status and progress parameters so that they can be sent to the UI. The **CalculationEventArgs** class is defined as follows.

```
public class CalculationEventArgs : EventArgs
    {
        public string          Result;
        public int             Progress;
        public CalculationStatus Status;

        public CalculationEventArgs( int progress )
        {
            this.Progress = progress;
            this.Status   = CalculationStatus.Calculating;
        }

        public CalculationEventArgs( CalculationStatus status )
        {
            this.Status = status;
        }
    }
```

The **StartCalculation** method is responsible for starting the calculation on the background thread. The delegate **CalculationDelegate** allows the **Calculation** method to be invoked on a background thread using the *Delegate Asynchronous Call* pattern, as shown in the following example.

```
public void StartCalculation( int count )
{
    lock( this )
    {
        if( _calcState == CalculationStatus.NotCalculating )
        {
            // Create a delegate to the calculation method.
            CalculationDelegate calc =
                    new CalculationDelegate( Calculation );

            // Start the calculation.
            calc.BeginInvoke( count,
                    new AsyncCallback( EndCalculate ), calc );

            // Update the calculation status.
            _calcState = CalculationStatus.Calculating;

            // Fire a status changed event.
            FireStatusChangedEvent( _calcState );
        }
    }
}
```

The **StopCalculation** method is responsible for canceling the calculation, as shown in the following code example.

```
public void StopCalculation()
{
    lock( this )
    {
        if( _calcState == CalculationStatus.Calculating )
        {
            // Update the calculation status.
            _calcState = CalculationStatus.CancelPending;

            // Fire a status changed event.
            FireStatusChangedEvent( _calcState );
        }
    }
}
```

When **StopCalculation** is called, the calculation state is set to **CancelPending** to signal the background to stop the calculation. An event is fired to the UI to signal that the cancel request has been received.

Both of these methods use the **lock** keyword to ensure that the changes to the calculation state variable are atomic, so your application does not encounter a race condition. Both methods fire a status changed event to inform the UI that the calculation is starting or stopping.

The calculation method is defined as follows.

```
private string Calculation( int count )
{
    string result = "";
    for ( int i = 0 ; i < count ; i++ )
    {
        // Long calculation...

        // Check for cancel.
        if ( _calcState == CalculationStatus.CancelPending ) break;

        // Update Progress
        FireProgressChangedEvent( count, i );
    }
    return result;
}
```

Note: For clarity, the details of the calculation have been omitted.

As each pass is made through the loop, the calculation state member is checked to see if the user has canceled the calculation. If so, the loop is exited, completing the calculation method. If the calculation continues, an event is fired, using the **FireProgressChanged** helper method, to report progress to the UI.

After the calculation is complete, the **EndCalculate** method is called to finish the asynchronous call by calling **EndInvoke**, as shown in the following example.

```
private void EndCalculate( IAsyncResult ar )
{
    CalculationDelegate del = (CalculationDelegate)ar.AsyncState;
    string result = del.EndInvoke( ar );

    lock( this )
    {
        _calcState = CalculationStatus.NotCalculating;
        FireStatusChangedEvent( _calcState );
    }
}
```

EndCalculate resets the calculation state to **NotCalculating**, ready for the next calculation to begin. It also fires a status changed event so that the UI can be notified that the calculation has been completed.

Using the Task Class

The **Task** class is responsible for managing background threads. To use the **Task** class, all you have to do is create a **Task** object, register the events that it fires, and implement the handling for these events. Because the events are fired on the UI thread, you don't need to worry about threading issues at all in your code.

The following example shows a **Task** object being created. In this example, the UI has two buttons, one for starting the calculation and one for stopping the calculation, and a progress bar that shows the current calculation progress.

```
// Create new task object to manage the calculation.
_calculationTask = new CalculationTask();

// Subscribe to the calculation status event.
_ calculationTask.CalculationStatusChanged += new
   CalculationTask.CalculationStatusEventHandler( OnCalculationStatusChanged );

// Subscribe to the calculation progress event.
_ calculationTask.CalculationProgressChanged += new
   CalculationTask.CalculationProgressEventHandler( OnCalculationProgressChanged );
```

The event handlers for the calculation status and calculation progress events update the UI appropriately, for example by updating a status bar control.

```
private void CalculationProgressChanged( object sender, CalculationEventArgs e )
{
    _progressBar.Value = e.Progress;
}
```

The **CalculationStatusChanged** event handler, which is shown in the following code, updates the value of a progress bar to reflect the current progress of the calculation. It is assumed that the minimum and maximum values of the progress bar have already been initialized.

```
private void CalculationStatusChanged( object sender, CalculationEventArgs e )
{
    switch ( e.Status )
    {
        case CalculationStatus.Calculating:
            button1.Enabled = false;
            button2.Enabled = true;
            break;

        case CalculationStatus.NotCalculating:
            button1.Enabled = true;
            button2.Enabled = false;
            break;

        case CalculationStatus.CancelPending:
            button1.Enabled = false;
            button2.Enabled = false;
            break;
    }
}
```

In this example, the **CalculationStatusChanged** event handler enables and disables the start and stop buttons depending on the calculation's status. This prevents the user from trying to start a calculation that is already in progress and provides feedback to the user about the status of the calculation.

The UI implements form event handlers for each button click to start and stop the calculation using the public methods on the **Task** object. For example, a start button event handler calls the **StartCalculation** method as follows.

```
private void startButton_Click( object sender, System.EventArgs e )
{
    calculationTask.StartCalculation( 1000 );
}
```

Similarly, a stop calculation button stops the calculation by calling the **StopCalculation** method as follows.

```
private void stopButton_Click( object sender, System.EventArgs e )
{
    calculationTask.StopCalculation();
}
```

Summary

Multithreading is an important part of creating responsive smart client applications. You should examine where multiple threads are appropriate for your application, looking to conduct all processing that does not involve the UI directly on separate threads. In most cases, you can use the **ThreadPool** class to create threads. However, in some cases you have to use the **Thread** class instead, and in others you need to use delegate objects or a Web service proxy to cause specific processing to occur on a non-UI thread.

In multithreaded applications, you must ensure that the UI thread is responsible for all UI-related tasks, and that you manage communication between the UI thread and other threads effectively. The *Task* pattern can help simplify this interaction significantly.

7

Deploying and Updating Smart Client Applications

Smart client applications perform local processing on the client computer, and so need to be deployed on those computers. In the past, deploying, updating, maintaining and uninstalling applications over time on client computers was difficult and problematic. With COM, several problems made it very difficult to deploy applications to the client computer, including:

- **Applications that were tightly coupled with the registry**. Installing a COM application required registering classes and type libraries in the registry.

- **Applications that were not self-contained**. Besides having to register classes and types in the registry, applications typically included shared files located on disk as well as configuration settings contained in the registry. The application wasn't self-contained; rather, its constituent parts were distributed to different areas on the computer.

- **Components that could not be deployed side by side**. It was not possible to deploy two different versions of the same DLL into the same directory.

These problems were a large barrier to effective deployment and maintenance of client applications.

The Microsoft® .NET Framework has a number of features that simplify the process of deploying .NET Framework applications. These features include:

- **Self-describing assemblies**. .NET Framework assemblies contain metadata that describes (among other things) version information, types, resources, and details of all referenced assemblies. This means that they are not dependent on the registry.

- **Versioning and side-by-side support**. The .NET Framework has extensive support for versioning, allowing you to install multiple versions of an application and multiple versions of the .NET Framework, so that they can run side by side.

- **Isolated applications**. .NET Framework assemblies can be deployed to the application directory, for use by that specific application, and by default are kept, isolated from other applications. This means that assemblies do not need to be deployed to the Windows directory or explicitly registered in the registry, and reduces the likelihood that they are overwritten or deleted when installing other applications.

- **Global assembly cache**. If you want to share code among different applications on the same computer, you can deploy components to the global assembly cache. The global assembly cache allows different versions of the same assembly to coexist. When referencing assemblies in the global assembly cache, you must specify the fully qualified name of the assembly that includes the public key token and version number. This helps prevent unintentional use of a different version of a component.

- **Default run-time binding against build-time assemblies for strong-named assemblies**. By default, if an assembly is strong named, the .NET Framework binds to the exact version of its dependent assemblies. This reduces application fragility because the .NET Framework loads the exact versions of the assemblies that it was built and tested against. This behavior can be explicitly overridden if required.

Collectively, these changes help to address many of the underlying issues that plagued the deployment and maintenance of rich client applications in the past. For more information about how the .NET Framework simplifies deployment, see "Simplifying Deployment and Solving DLL Hell with the .NET Framework" at *http://msdn.microsoft.com/library/default.asp?url=/library/en-us/dndotnet/html/dplywithnet.asp*.

This chapter describes the options for deploying the .NET Framework itself, and then examines how to deploy smart client applications based on the .NET Framework. There are a number of options for deploying your applications, and each is discussed, followed by a discussion in selecting the method most appropriate for your environment. Finally the options for deploying application updates are examined in some detail.

Deploying the .NET Framework

.NET smart client applications rely on the .NET Framework to function, and therefore require it to be deployed on the client computer. The .NET Framework is deployed using the.NET Framework redistributable package, which can be obtained from Microsoft MSDN® or the Windows Update Web site.

You can also obtain the redistributable package from a product CD or DVD. The package is available on the .NET Framework SDK, and on the Microsoft Visual Studio® .NET 2003 DVD.

The .NET Framework redistributable package is actually a Windows Installer package that is wrapped into a single, self-extracting executable file named Dotnetfx.exe. The Dotnetfx.exe executable file starts Install.exe, which performs platform checks, installs Windows Installer version 2.0 if necessary, and then starts the Windows Installer package (.msi file).

For more information about using Dotnetfx.exe, see ".NET Framework Redistributable Package 1.1 Technical Reference" at *http://msdn.microsoft.com /library/default.asp?url=/library/en-us/dnnetdep/html/dotnetfxref1_1.asp*.

Preinstalling the .NET Framework

Today, many enterprises choose to deploy the .NET Framework as part of their standard operating environment. You can deploy the .NET Framework across your enterprise in two ways:

- **Use technologies for pushing software to client computers**, such as the Group Policy functionality of Microsoft Active Directory® directory service, or Microsoft Systems Management Server (SMS). Using Group Policy software deployment to install the package over the network allows you to ensure that the package is installed with elevated privileges. Similarly, using an enterprise push technology such as SMS allows you to install the .NET Framework with the required permissions. To install the .NET Framework using Group Policy or SMS, you first need to extract the Windows Installer file from dotnetfx.exe. For more details about how to do this, see "Redistributing the .NET Framework" at *http://msdn.microsoft.com/library/default.asp?url=/library/en-us/dnnetdep/html /redistdeploy.asp*.

- **Require that end users deploy the .NET Framework themselves** by using Windows Update, or by downloading the .NET Framework from a network share, an internal Web site, or the Microsoft Web site. End users will need to have administrative privileges on their computers to deploy the .NET Framework because the .NET Framework Redistributable Package setup program requires administrative privileges to install.

Installing the .NET Framework with an Application

In cases where you cannot determine which computers have the .NET Framework preinstalled, you may choose to install the .NET Framework only when it is required — in other words, when a .NET Framework application is installed. This approach is particularly useful when you do not know the exact software configurations of the computers you will be deploying to, and hence do not know if the .NET Framework is preinstalled or not. For example, if you are an independent software vendor (ISV) developing and packaging your smart client application for sale to a wide variety of customers, you may not know whether or not your customers' computers have the .NET Framework installed.

To ensure that the .NET Framework is installed along with your application, you can use the setup.exe Bootstrapper sample. This sample checks to see if the .NET Framework has already been installed, and if it hasn't, the sample then installs the .NET Framework before installing the application.

For more information about using the setup.exe Bootstrapper sample, see Chapter 3 of *Deploying .NET Framework-based Applications* at *http://www.microsoft.com/downloads /details.aspx?FamilyId=5B7C6E2D-D03F-4B19-9025-6B87E6AE0DA6&displaylang=en*.

Deploying Smart Client Applications

As you design your smart client applications, you should consider how those applications will be deployed. Wherever possible, you should try to minimize the system impact of any installation. Doing so allows you to keep closer track of any changes to the application and eases the problems of updating and uninstalling applications. However, sometimes you will need to perform more complex installations, for example when you are reusing unmanaged code components, or when you need to store sensitive data securely in the registry.

A number of options are available to you when deploying smart client applications. These include:

- **No-touch deployment**. With this approach, you copy the files to a Web server, and the .NET Framework will automatically download the application and its dependent assemblies to the client when the user clicks a link.

- **No-touch deployment with an application update stub**. With this approach, you use no-touch deployment to download an application stub, which then downloads the rest of the application to the local disk.

- **Running code from a file share**. With this approach, you copy the files to a file share and run the application from the share.

- **Xcopy**. With this approach, you copy the files directly to the client. The .NET Framework allows the application and all of its dependent assemblies to be located in a single directory structure, so you don't need to register anything on the client.

- **Windows Installer packages**. With this approach, you package your application's files in a Windows Installer package, and the package is then installed on the client.

Each approach has its own strengths and weaknesses. To help determine the most appropriate deployment approach for your environment, you should examine each in more detail.

No-Touch Deployment

No-touch deployment allows your users to access your application on a Web server by using a URL link to the application. To deploy an application by using no-touch deployment, you simply need to copy the appropriate files to the Web server. When a user browses to the location of the application by using a URL link, Microsoft Internet Explorer downloads and runs the application. The application and its dependent assemblies are downloaded to the client by using HTTP and are stored in a special location called the assembly download cache. When the .NET Framework determines whether or not an assembly on the Web server needs to be downloaded, only the date-time stamp on the file is checked, and not the assembly version number. If the assemblies on the server do not have a later date-time stamp than those on the client, they will not be downloaded.

If you use no-touch deployment to deploy your smart client applications, you need to provide the user with a URL to the location of the application on the Web server. With this approach, no installation program is necessary on the client computer — all code is downloaded as needed. Your application is automatically updated whenever changes occur on the Web server. If files have changed, the newer versions are downloaded as needed, just as with normal Web browsing.

No-touch deployment depends on the ability of the .NET Framework to interact with Internet Explorer 5.01 or later to check for .NET assemblies that are being requested. During a request, the executable file is downloaded to the download cache. A process named **IEExec** then launches the application in a secure isolated environment provided by the code access security infrastructure of the .NET Framework.

Note: The client will attempt to run the application only if it has both the .NET Framework and Internet Explorer version 5.01 or later installed.

If you decide to use no-touch deployment to deploy an application that uses application configuration files, you may need to configure the Web server directory to allow for the download of the application's configuration files, because this capability is not enabled by default. Be sure to enable configuration files to be downloaded only from the directory in which your application is located; otherwise, you may enable private configuration files to be downloaded and introduce a security risk.

Note: Configuration files are actually downloaded twice when no-touch deployment is used: the first time to check for binding information (for example, to control the exact versions of components that the application uses) and the second to look for user-specific configuration information.

You can use no-touch deployment from within an application that is already deployed to download and run code by using the **Assembly.LoadFrom()** method. This technique can be used to download code that changes frequently, such as business rules that change frequently, or to provide on-demand installation of some other functionality.

No-touch deployment allows you to run localized versions of the application. The current culture of the client computer is used to automatically download the appropriate resource assemblies required to provide a localized version of the application.

You can secure no-touch deployment applications by using the security mechanisms provided by the Web server. For example, to restrict access to the application to authorized users on an intranet, you can enable Windows Integrated Security on the application directory on the Web server. To allow all users to access the application, you can enable anonymous access to the application's directory.

Note: If your Web server does not allow anonymous access or use Windows Integrated Security to authenticate clients, your application may not be able to download the configuration file.

Limitations of No-Touch Deployment

No-touch deployment can be useful for deploying simple applications, or for deploying parts of a more complex application. However, it is not an appropriate deployment approach for the full installation of more complex smart client applications for the following reasons:

- Restricted default security settings
- Unreliable offline functionality
- No transacted installations

Note: The ClickOnce technology in version 2.0 of the .NET Framework will remove the need to manually make security policy changes to the client before the application is installed and run. ClickOnce will provide a configurable mechanism to allow security policy changes to be made automatically when the application is first installed from the Web server. ClickOnce will also provide reliable offline functionality to smart client applications and will allow them to be fully integrated with the Windows Shell.

This section examines the restrictions of no-touch deployment in more detail.

Restricted Default Security Settings

Code access security grants permissions to the application according to the evidence that the application presents. By default, the application's location (the URL from where it was started) is used to determine the permissions that it is granted. Unless local security policy on the client computer is changed, no-touch deployment applications are partially trusted, which means that they are only granted a limited number of permissions.

By default, a smart client application deployed using no-touch deployment will not be able to do the following:

- Write to the hard disk (except to isolated storage)
- Deploy assemblies to the global assembly cache
- Deploy or use unmanaged code
- Deploy components that require registration or make other registry changes
- Integrate with the Windows Shell (specifically, the install icons on the **Start** menu and the **Add or Remove Programs** item in Control Panel)
- Access a database
- Interact with any other client applications, such as Microsoft Office applications
- Access Web services or other network-located resources that are not located on the same server on which the application is deployed
- Perform other security operations outside those defined in the zone associated with the deployment location

If your application requires more than the default set of permissions and you want to use no-touch deployment, you will have to modify the security policy on the client to grant the application the permissions to function properly. Such security policy changes need to be propagated to client computers before you deploy your application (for example, using Group Policy, a Windows Installer package, or a batch file). These requirements reduce some of the benefits of the no-touch deployment approach. For more information about deploying security policy, see ".NET Framework Enterprise Security Policy Administration and Deployment" at *http://msdn.microsoft.com/library/default.asp?url=/library/en-us/dnnetsec/html /entsecpoladmin.asp*.

As you design your applications, you should determine whether you can meet the design specifications of your smart client application and comply with the partial trust requirements of a no-touch deployment application. In general, no-touch deployment and running code from a file share offer solutions that are easy to deploy, but may restrict the functionality of the application to such an extent that they are impractical for many smart client applications. However, if your application does not require any additional permission, no-touch deployment may be an ideal deployment mechanism for your application.

For more information about fully trusted and partially trusted applications, see Chapter 4, "Security Considerations."

Unreliable Offline Functionality

Another problem with deploying smart client applications using no-touch deployment is that they do not function reliably offline. This problem is due to a number of factors:

- **Delayed downloading of assemblies**. Assemblies are downloaded on demand and are stored in the assembly download cache, which is managed as part of the Internet Explorer cache. In some cases, when you run the application online, you may not download all parts of the application, which will affect the application's ability to function fully when offline.

- **Assemblies may be deleted**. Because the assemblies reside in an area managed by the Internet Explorer cache, if the cache is flushed for any reason, your application files will be deleted.

- **Applications are dependent on Internet Explorer offline settings**. When attempting to run an application offline, you must set Internet Explorer to run in offline mode, even though your application does not run within Internet Explorer. Also, if you do have connectivity, but Internet Explorer is inadvertently set to offline mode, no checks for updates will be made to the server.

No Transacted Installations

With no-touch deployment, assemblies are downloaded when required to a cache that can be flushed at any time. It is therefore not possible to be sure at any time that all of the necessary code is installed on the local disk. For many organizations, this uncertainty may be unacceptable for line-of-business applications.

No-Touch Deployment with an Application Update Stub

One of the main problems with using no-touch deployment is that, by default, the application runs from the assembly download cache, and under partial trust, unless the local security policy is modified. This can limit the functionality of your smart client application, including its ability to function reliably offline. One way to circumvent this problem is to use no-touch deployment initially to deploy an application stub, which in turn automatically downloads and installs the rest of the application to the local disk. The stub deploys the application to a specified location on disk, such as "C:\Program Files", and is therefore not subject to the limitations of the Internet Explorer cache. When the application is run, it will be granted full trust permissions because it is being run from the local disk, and can operate without the restrictions associated with partial trust applications. An application update stub can also be used to ensure that the application is reliably and automatically updated if changes occur on the server.

If you use this method to deploy your application, you need to ensure that the .NET Framework security policy of the client computer is modified to allow the application stub itself to run with sufficient permissions to download and store the application artifacts on the local disk.

Designing application update stubs can be complex. To help you, Microsoft has created the Updater Application Block, which you can use as a basis for designing your own automatic updates solution. The Updater Application Block is designed to:

- Implement a pull-based update solution for .NET Framework applications.
- Use cryptographic validation techniques to verify the authenticity of application updates before applying them.
- Perform post-deployment configuration tasks without user intervention.
- Help you write applications that automatically update themselves to the latest available version.

The architecture of the Updater Application Block is shown in Figure 7.1.

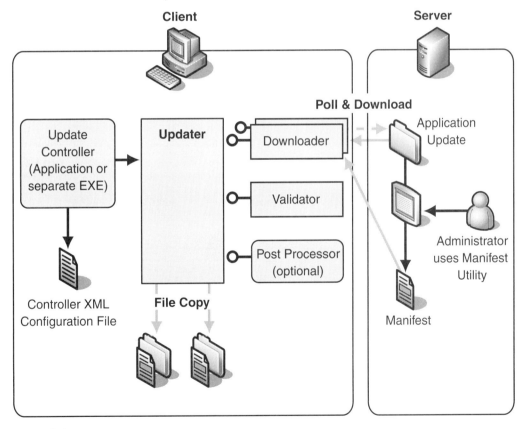

Figure 7.1
Updater Application Block architecture

For more information about the Updater Application Block, see "Updater Application Block for .NET" at *http://msdn.microsoft.com/library/default.asp?url=/library/en-us/dnbda /html/updater.asp.*

No-touch deployment with an application update stub supports the transacted installation of your application. The Updater Application Block can help ensure that the application is installed successfully in its entirety. To perform a transacted installation, you will need to include code that, in addition to performing the automatic updates, checks to see that all code has been installed on the local disk. This code can be in the form of a manifest file along with code that determines that each file in the manifest is on the local disk.

Combining no-touch deployment with an application update stub gives you many of the benefits of simplified deployment and updates as well as the ability to run your application in a fully trusted environment. Such benefits make this hybrid approach a useful choice for the deployment of many smart client applications. However, it is not the ideal choice in all situations. You still need to grant the application stub sufficient permissions to allow the stub to download the rest of the application. Also, applications installed using this approach do not provide Windows Shell integration (specifically, integration with the **Start** menu or the **Add or Remove Programs** item in Control Panel) unless you build this functionality into the application stub. Finally, the deployment and updates will only occur under the security context of user. This restriction can cause problems if your application needs to write to the registry, or to a part of the file system that you secure from the user.

Running Code from a File Share

Running code from a file share is similar to no-touch deployment, except that you provide users with a file share, rather than a URL, from which to deploy and run the application. Code run from a file share is downloaded on demand and is executed as appropriate. Because the code is running from the network, it runs as a partially trusted application, generally running from the local intranet and receiving the local intranet permission set, unless you change the security policy on the client.

Running code from a file share has many of the advantages and disadvantages of no-touch deployment, although the code is not cached on the client as it is with no-touch deployment. Because of the security restrictions associated with running code from a file share, it is often not appropriate for deploying smart client applications.

Note: As with no-touch deployment, you can adopt a hybrid approach that combines running code from a file share with an automatic update stub. For more information, see "No-Touch Deployment with an Application Update Stub" earlier in this chapter.

Xcopy Deployment

Xcopy deployment entails copying all of the files that the application consists of to the client computer so that the application can be run. Smart client applications often just consist of one or more executable files, one or more DLLs, and one or more configuration files located in a directory hierarchy. By copying all of these files to another computer, you essentially install the application. To uninstall the application, you just remove all of the files from the computer.

In situations where you only need to modify the file system to install the application, the **Xcopy** approach may be the best option. However, because you do not have programmatic control over the installation process, the **Xcopy** approach does *not* allow you to do the following:

- Deploy assemblies to the global assembly cache (and maintain references).
- Deploy COM objects.
- Deploy components that require registration or make other registry changes.
- Integrate with the Windows Shell.

If your application requires additional installation steps, you may be able to perform these steps manually after copying the files. For example, if you need to modify the registry, you can edit the registry on your target computer or import *.reg files to ensure that the appropriate settings are in place. If you need to deploy assemblies to the global assembly cache, you can use the Gacutil.exe utility with the **/ir** switch, which installs assemblies into the global assembly cache with a traced reference. These references can be removed when the assembly is uninstalled by using the **/ur** switch.

Note: You can also use a drag-and-drop operation in Windows Explorer to move shared assemblies into the Global Assembly Cache folder. However, you should avoid this method because it does not implement reference counting. Without reference counting, the uninstall routine of another application can cause an assembly required by your application to be removed from the global assembly cache.

Xcopy deployment is suitable for some smart client applications, but in many cases the additional steps required to get the application to function properly makes this seemingly simple approach too laborious.

Windows Installer Packages

You can package your application for installation as a Windows Installer package. This approach gives you the unrestricted ability to install anything on the target computer, although the application is limited at run time by the security context of the end user installing the application.

Windows Installer packages are very flexible and powerful, so you can use them to install very complex applications that make a large number of configuration changes to the client. However, they are also appropriate for applications with much simpler installation requirements. Even if you have designed your application to have minimal impact on the client when installed, you should consider using Windows Installer packages, because they integrate with the Windows Shell by adding icons on the **Start** menu and desktop and adding the application to the **Add or Remove Programs** item in Control Panel. This integration allows you to control the installation effectively and uninstall the application when required.

You can add any or all of the following to a Windows Installer package:

- Project output groups
- Services files and folders
- Assemblies
- Application resources
- Merge modules
- CAB files
- Dependencies
- Registry settings
- Project properties
- Custom actions
- User interface design settings

After you have created a Windows Installer package, you have a number of options for distributing it to the client computer, including:

- Using enterprise push technologies such as SMS
- Using the Group Policy functionality of Active Directory to publish or assign the packages
- Allowing users to install the package from media, a file share, or a URL

Using a push technology to install your Windows Installer packages allows you to have some centralized control over when and where the installation occurs. It also allows you to control which groups within the enterprise should have the application, or particular versions of the application. You can, for example, ensure that the installation occurs at a particular time of day for a particular group of users. However, bear in mind that you may require significant hardware and network bandwidth, depending on the size of your applications, to ensure that large-scale deployments work effectively.

One of the most significant advantages of a Windows Installer package is that if you use Group Policy or SMS, you can install the application without the user requiring administrative permissions. Windows Installer packages also automatically support transacted installations. Either all of the files and configuration changes will be installed by a Windows Installer package, or, if there is a problem, the installation will be rolled back in its entirety by Windows Installer.

The flexibility of the Windows Installer package means that it can be appropriate for installations of any complexity, from applications that simply write to the file system and integrate with the **Add or Remove Programs** item in Control Panel, to those that make many significant configuration changes to the client.

Note: If you use Windows Installer packages to deploy your application; you do not have to use the same method to deploy updates. In many cases it is preferable to design your application to automatically update itself after it is installed. For more details about configuring your applications for automatic updates, see "Automatic Updates" later in this chapter.

Choosing the Right Deployment Approach

With so many deployment choices available for smart client applications, it can be challenging to determine the correct choice for your environment. However, the requirements of your application and the needs of your users will normally determine the best approach.

The following table summarizes the features of each deployment approach.

Table 7.1: Deployment Approaches for Smart Client Applications

	No touch deployment	No-touch deployment with application update stub	Running code from a file share	Xcopy deployment	Windows Installer package
Reliable offline access	No	Yes	No	Yes	Yes
Full trust application functionality	Requires client security policy changes	Yes	Requires client security policy changes	Yes	Yes

(continued)

Table 7.1: Deployment Approaches for Smart Client Applications *(continued)*

	No touch deployment	No-touch deployment with application update stub	Running code from a file share	Xcopy deployment	Windows Installer package
Non-power user installation	Yes	Depends on requirements of application	Yes	Yes	Depends on requirements of application and application distribution mechanism
Low system impact	Yes	Depends on requirements of application	Yes	Yes	Depends on requirements of application
Windows Shell integration	No	No	No	No	Yes
Unrestricted installation	No	No	No	No	Yes
Transacted installation	No	Yes	No	No	Yes
Need to modify .NET Framework security policy of the client	Yes — if client needs to run under elevated permissions	Yes — for application stub only.	Yes — if client needs to run under elevated permissions	No	No

In many cases the simplest approach is to package your application using a Windows Installer package. Windows Installer packages are highly flexible and allow you to install applications of any complexity. If you use an enterprise push technology such as Group Policy or SMS to deploy your Windows Installer package, you can also install the applications under an administrative security context, regardless of the security context of the user. No-touch deployment with an automatic update stub is also a viable option when you want to allow your users to install their application by clicking a URL, but you will have to make changes to the local security policy of the target computer to ensure that your application stub application can run under full trust.

Deploying Smart Client Updates

After you have initially deployed your smart client applications, your work is not done. The applications will need to be updated over time, as you upgrade application functionality and fix bugs or address security vulnerabilities.

Depending on the situation, you may or may not use the same approach to update a smart client application as you used to deploy it. For example, if you initially deploy an application using a Windows Installer package, you may use automatic updates to deploy updates. The specifics of your environment will often determine which update methodology is most appropriate.

One common requirement when deploying updates is the ability to federate the update infrastructure, so that updates do not run off a single server or server farm controlled by a single entity. For example, if an ISV has created a smart client application that is deployed across a customer's enterprise, and the ISV releases an update for the application, the enterprise may want to download and test that update in their standard operating environment before it is propagated to all computers running across the enterprise. Federating the update infrastructure makes it possible to do so. For example, an update server could exist on the customer site that is responsible for obtaining updates from the ISV. The clients running within the enterprise would obtain the updates from the local update server, but only when the IT administrators approved it. This approach can also be used to increase the performance and scalability of the update infrastructure by relieving load of a single server or server farm.

When deploying updates to an application, you have the following options:

- **No-touch deployment**. The updated assemblies are added to the Web server for automatic download by the clients.
- **Automatic updates**. The application is configured to automatically download and install updates from a server.
- **Updates from a file share**. The updated assemblies are added to a network share for automatic download by the clients.
- **Xcopy updates**. The updates are copied directly to the clients.
- **Windows Installer package deployment**. The Windows Installer package is updated, a new package is created, or a patch package is used to update the client.

It is useful to examine each of the options in more detail so that you can determine which is most appropriate for your environment.

No-Touch Deployment Updates

If you have used no-touch deployment to deploy a simple application or parts of a more complex application, you can update these assemblies simply by placing the new files on the Web server. Before an assembly is loaded by the application, the .NET Framework automatically checks the time stamp of the assembly locally and on the Web server to see whether the assembly needs to be downloaded again, or whether the assembly can simply be run from the user's assembly download cache.

Note: No-touch deployment has a number of restrictions that make it unsuitable for deploying most smart client applications. For more details, see "No-Touch Deployment" earlier in this chapter.

Although issuing updates using a no-touch deployment method is generally very straightforward, your clients can have problems during an upgrade due to the lack of support for transacted installations. If you update the directory while clients are using the application, a client might download old code initially and then attempt to download other code that has since been updated. This can lead to unpredictable results and may cause your application to fail. The simplest solution to this problem is to deploy any significant updates to a separate directory on the Web server, and when deployment is complete, to change any links to the new location.

Note: If you choose to deploy your application using no-touch deployment with an automatic update stub, see the following section, "Automatic Updates."

Automatic Updates

In most cases, the best approach for patching, repackaging, and updating applications is to build the updating infrastructure into the application itself. In this case, the client application can be designed to automatically download and install updates from a server, and the IT administrator releases these updates to the server for clients to obtain. To achieve this, you can include code with an application so that the application does the following:

- Automatically checks for updates.
- Downloads updates if available.
- Upgrades itself by applying those updates.

As you configure your application for automatic updates, it is important to ensure that all of the updated files are downloaded to the client. This is particularly important when you update strong-named assemblies. Assemblies that call strong-named assemblies must specify the version of the strong-named assembly, so if you update strong-named assemblies, you must also update any assemblies that call them.

When configuring transacted updates, you can use code to check that the updates are installed locally, verifying them against a manifest. Often you will decide to install the update in a separate directory, and then either remove the original directory after a successful installation, or leave the original directory in place to provide a fallback application.

For more details about automatic updates and the use of the Updater Application Block, see "No-Touch Deployment with an Application Update Stub" earlier in this chapter.

Note: Automatic updates will be simplified with the ClickOnce feature in version 2.0 of the .NET Framework. As part of a deployment manifest, you will be able to specify whether and when the application should check for updates, along with an alternate update location.

Updates from a File Share

When you copy assemblies to a file share, those assemblies are downloaded to the client each time the application runs and are not cached. As with no-touch deployment, updating an application that was originally deployed by running code from a file share is simply a matter of adding the new code to the file share. The client then downloads the new code the next time it runs.

Xcopy Updates

If you originally distributed your application using a file copy technique, you may want to deploy updates in the same way. Regardless of the original deployment mechanism, though, file copy can be one of the most effective approaches for updating your application when the updates are relatively simple, such as modifications to a configuration file. In such cases, deploying an update is simply a matter of copying the new files and removing any old files that are no longer required.

Usually you can update private assemblies by simply copying the new version of the assembly over the old one. However, although you can use simple copy operations for the initial deployment of a strong-named assembly, it is not possible to update the strong-named assembly in this way and have your application (or other assemblies) use it automatically. The strong name of the assembly is stored in the manifest of any assembly that references it, and different versions of a strong-named assembly are considered to be completely separate assemblies by the common language runtime (CLR). Unless you specify otherwise, the CLR loads the same version of the strong-named assembly that your application was originally built against.

Windows Installer Updates

Windows Installer offers a comprehensive solution for updating .NET Framework applications. Several of its features are specifically designed to solve application update problems.

Windows Installer packages have built-in support for version control. If you version your application correctly, the Windows Installer package can automatically ensure that the update happens correctly, and you can specify whether previous versions of the application are to be removed when the new application is installed.

If you are using a push technology, such as SMS, to deploy these updates, you can also control which users receive updates and when they receive them. This feature is particularly useful if you are testing updates with a particular group of people before deploying the updates more extensively.

If you plan to upgrade your application using Windows Installer technology, you have three choices for implementing the upgrade:

- Build a patch package (.msp) and apply it to the currently installed application.
- Update the existing Windows Installer file.
- Create a completely new Windows Installer file.

In general, if you are going to use Windows Installer to deploy updates, you should use either use a patch package or update the existing Windows Installer file. If you create an entirely new Windows Installer file, the Microsoft Windows® operating system will not recognize the package as an update, and the upgrade management features of Windows will not function properly. However, in some cases, the changes are so extensive that you may choose to forego this functionality and create a new Windows Installer file.

Note: For more information about deploying updates using Windows Installer, see *Deploying .NET Framework-Based Applications* at *http://www.microsoft.com/downloads /details.aspx?FamilyId=5B7C6E2D-D03F-4B19-9025-6B87E6AE0DA6&displaylang=en*.

Choosing the Right Update Approach

In some cases, the update approach you choose is defined by the deployment approach you chose for your application. However, the most appropriate approach is often determined by the nature of the updates that you are deploying. For example, you may just be copying new files over old ones, or you may want the updated application to run alongside the old one. The update may involve adding new assemblies to the global assembly cache or changing configuration information in the registry. The updates are further complicated if you are deploying updates to strong-named assemblies, because each assembly that calls the strong-named assembly will use the version number in the call.

Table 7.2 summarizes the options available for updating your applications and the features that each support.

Table 7.2: Update Approaches for Smart Client Applications

	No-touch deployment updates	Automatic updates with an application update stub	Updates from a file share	Xcopy updates	Windows Installer updates
Non-power user update	Yes	Depends on requirements of application	Yes	No	Depends on requirements of application and application distribution mechanism
Centralized management of updates	Yes	Yes	Yes	No	Depends on application distribution mechanism
Updates downloaded when application is run	Yes	Yes	No	No	No
Federated update infrastructure	No	Yes	No	No	Yes
Per user/group updates	Yes	Yes	No	No	Depends on application distribution mechanism
Transacted updates	No	Yes	No	No	Yes
Built-in support for version control	No	No	No	No	Yes

In many cases, automatic updates are the most effective approach for deploying updates for your application. However, when deploying major updates, or updates that involve complex configuration changes to the client, you may need to use Windows Installer, which also has the benefit of automatic version control support.

Summary

Deploying smart client applications is much easier than deploying rich client applications was in the past, due to the features of the .NET Framework. However, there are a number of important choices you need to make for successful deployment, both in how you design your application for easy deployment, and in which deployment approach you choose for the application and for the .NET Framework itself.

In most cases, the best choice for deploying the application is either to use a Windows Installer package, or to use a combination of no-touch deployment and an application update stub. You will need to consider how to maintain the application and deploy updates effectively after it is deployed. Again, in most cases, the best choice is likely to be either Windows Installer, or automated updates, controlled by the application itself.

8

Smart Client
Application Performance

Smart client applications can provide a richer and more responsive user interface than Web applications can, and can take advantage of local system resources. If a large portion of the application resides on the user's computer, the application does not require constant round trips to a Web server. This can result in an increase in performance and responsiveness. However, to realize the full potential of a smart client application, you should carefully consider performance issues during the application's design phase. Addressing performance issues when you architect and design your application can help you contain costs early and reduce the likelihood of running into performance problems later on.

Note: Improving the performance of smart client applications is not limited to application design issues. There are a number of steps that you can take throughout the application lifecycle to make .NET code perform well. Although the .NET common language runtime (CLR) is very efficient at executing code, there a number of techniques that you can use to increase the performance of your code and prevent performance problems from being introduced at the code level. For more information on these issues, see *http://msdn.microsoft.com/perf*.

Defining realistic performance requirements and identifying potential issues in the design of your application is clearly important, but often performance problems appear only after the code has been written, and is being tested. In this case, there are tools and techniques that can help you track down performance problems.

This chapter examines how to how to design and tune your smart client applications for optimum performance. It discusses a number of design and architectural issues, including threading and caching considerations, and examines how to enhance the performance of the Windows Forms portions of your application. The chapter also looks at some of the techniques and tools that you can use to track down and diagnose performance problems with your smart client applications.

Designing for Performance

There are many things you can do at an application design or architectural level to ensure that a smart client application performs well. You should make sure to set realistic and measurable performance goals as early as possible in the design phase, which allows you to evaluate design tradeoffs and provide the most cost effective way to address performance issues. Wherever possible, performance goals should be based on real user and business requirements because these are strongly influenced by the environment in which your application operates. Performance modeling is a structured and repeatable process you can use to manage and ensure your application meets the performance goals. For more information, see Chapter 2, "Performance Modeling" in *Improving .NET Application Performance and Scalability*, at *http://msdn.microsoft.com/library/default.asp?url=/library/en-us/dnpag/html /scalenetchapt02.asp*.

Smart clients are usually part of a larger distributed application. It is important to consider the performance of the smart client application in the context of the complete application, including all of the network-located resources that the client application uses. Fine tuning and optimizing every single component in an application is usually not required or possible. Instead, your performance tuning should be based on priorities, time, budget constraints, and risks. Pursuing high performance for its own sake is not usually a cost-effective strategy.

Smart clients will also need to coexist with other applications on your user's computers. As you design your smart client applications, you should take into account the fact that your applications will need to share system resources such as memory, CPU time, and network utilization with the other applications on the client computer.

Note: Information concerning the design of scalable, high performance remote services can be found in *Improving .NET Performance and Scalability*, at *http://msdn.microsoft.com/library/default.asp?url= /library/en-us/dnpag/html/scalenet.asp*. The guide contains detailed information about how to optimize your .NET code for best performance.

To design smart clients to perform efficiently, consider the following:

- **Caching data where appropriate**. Data caching can dramatically improve the performance of a smart client application, allowing you to work with data locally rather than having to retrieve it from the network constantly. However, data that is sensitive or changes frequently is not usually appropriate for caching.

- **Optimizing network communications**. Communication through chatty interfaces to remote tier services with multiple request/response round trips to perform a single logical operation can consume system and network resources, resulting in poor application performance.

- **Using threads efficiently**. If you use a user interface (UI) thread to perform blocking I/O bound calls, the UI may seem unresponsive to the user. Creating a large number of unnecessary threads can result in poor performance because of the overhead of creating and shutting down threads.

- **Using transactions efficiently**. If the client has local data, then using atomic transactions can help you to ensure that that data is consistent. Because the data is local, the transaction is also local rather than distributed. For smart clients that are working offline, any changes made to the local data are tentative. The client needs to synchronize the changes when it goes online again. For data that is not local, it is possible to use distributed transactions in some cases (for example when services are in the same physical location with good connectivity and where the service supports it). Services such as Web services and Message Queuing do not support distributed transactions.

- **Optimizing application startup time**. Fast application startup time allows the user to begin interacting with the application more quickly, which gives the user an immediate and favorable perception of application performance and usability. Your application should be designed so that only those assemblies that are required are loaded on application startup. Avoid using large numbers of assemblies because loading each assembly incurs a performance cost.

- **Managing available resources efficiently**. Poor design decisions, such as implementing finalizers when they are not needed, failing to suppress finalization in the **Dispose** method, or failing to release unmanaged resources, can lead to unnecessary delays in reclaiming resources and can create resource leaks that degrade application performance. Applications that fail to properly release resources, or explicitly force garbage collection, can prevent the CLR from efficiently managing memory.

- **Optimizing Windows Forms performance**. Smart client applications rely on Windows Forms to provide a rich and responsive user interface. There are a number of techniques you can use to ensure that Windows Forms provide optimal performance. These include reducing the complexity of the user interface, and avoiding loading large amounts of data at once.

In many cases the perceived performance of your application from the user's perspective is at least as important as the actual performance of the application. You can create an application that appears to perform much more efficiently to the user by making certain changes to your design, such as using background asynchronous processing (to keep the UI responsive), showing a progress bar to indicate the progress of tasks, and providing the option for users to cancel long running tasks.

These issues are discussed in more detail in throughout this section.

Data Caching Guidelines

Caching is an important technique to improve application performance and provide a responsive user interface. You should consider the following options:

- **Caching frequently retrieved data to reduce roundtrips**. If your application has to interact frequently with a network service to retrieve data, you should consider caching that data on the client, reducing the need to obtain the data repeatedly over the network. This can increase performance substantially, providing near instantaneous access to the data, and removing the risk of network delays and outages that can adversely affect the performance of your smart client application.

- **Caching read-only reference data**. Read-only reference data is usually an ideal candidate for caching. Such data is used to provide data for validation and user interface display purposes, such as product descriptions, IDs, and so on. Because this kind of data cannot be changed by the client, it can usually be cached without any further special handling on the client.

- **Caching data that is to be sent to network-located services**. You should consider caching data that is to be sent to a network-located service. For example, if your application allows users to enter order information that consists of a number of discrete items of data gathered over a number of forms, consider allowing the user to enter all of the data, and then send it in one network call at the end of the entry process.

- **Minimizing caching of highly volatile data**. Before you can cache any volatile data, you need to consider how long it can be cached before it becomes stale or otherwise unusable. If data is highly volatile and your application relies on up-to-date information, it is likely that the data can only be cached for a short time, if at all.

- **Minimizing caching of sensitive data**. You should avoid caching sensitive data on the client because, in most cases, you cannot guarantee the physical security of the client. However, if you do cache sensitive data on the client, you will generally need to encrypt the data, which has its own performance implications.

Further issues surrounding data caching are covered in more detail in Chapter 2 of this guide. Also see the "Caching" section of *Improving .NET Application Performance and Scalability*, Chapter 3, "Design Guidelines for Application Performance" (*http://msdn.microsoft.com/library/default.asp?url=/library/en-us/dnpag/html /scalenetchapt03.asp*) and *Improving .NET Application Performance and Scalability*, Chapter 4, "Architecture and Design Review of .NET Application for Performance and Scalability" (*http://msdn.microsoft.com/library/default.asp?url=/library/en-us/dnpag /html/scalenetchapt04.asp*).

Network Communications Guidelines

Another decision you will face is how to design and work with network services, such as Web services. In particular, you should consider the granularity, synchronicity, and frequency of interaction with network services. For the best performance and scalability, you should send more data in a single call rather than send smaller amounts of data in several calls. For example, if your application allows users to enter multiple items in a purchase order, it is better to collect data for all items, and then to send the completed purchase order to the service at one time, rather than send individual item details in multiple calls. In addition to reducing the overhead associated with making many network calls, this also reduces the need for complex state management within the service and/or the client.

Your smart client applications should be designed to use asynchronous communication whenever possible, as this will help to keep the user interface responsive and execute tasks in parallel. For more information on how to initiate calls and retrieve data asynchronously using **BeginInvoke** and **EndInvoke** methods see, "Asynchronous Programming Overview" (*http://msdn.microsoft.com/library /default.asp?url=/library/en-us/cpguide/html/cpovrasynchronousprogrammingoverview.asp*).

Note: For more information on designing and building smart client applications that are occasionally connected to the network, see Chapter 3, "Getting Connected" and Chapter 4, "Occasionally Connected Smart Clients."

Threading Guidelines

Using multiple threads within your application can be a good way to increase its responsiveness and performance. In particular, you should consider using threads to carry out processing that can safely be done in the background and that does not require user interaction. Performing such work in the background allows the user to continue working with the application and allows the application's main user-interface thread to maintain the application's responsiveness.

Good candidates for processing that can be done on a separate thread include:

- **Application Initialization**. Perform lengthy initialization on a background thread so that the user is able to interact with your application as soon as possible, especially if an important or major part of the application functionality does not depend on this initialization completing.

- **Remote Service Calls**. Make all remote calls over the network on a separate background thread. It is difficult — if not impossible — to guarantee response times for services located on the network. Performing these calls on a separate thread reduces the risk of network outages or slowdowns adversely affecting application performance.

- **IO Bound Processing**. Processing, such as searching and sorting data on disk, should be done on a separate thread. Typically, this kind of work is subject to the constraints of the disk I/O sub-system, and not processor availability, so your application can effectively maintain its responsiveness while this work is carried out in the background.

While the performance benefits of using multiple threads can be significant, it is important to note that threads consume resources of their own and using too many threads can create a burden on the processor, which needs to manage context switching between threads. To prevent this, consider using a thread pool instead of creating and managing your own threads. Thread pools will efficiently manage the threads for you, reusing existing thread objects and minimizing the overhead associated with thread creation and disposal.

If the user experience is impacted by work performed by background threads, you should always keep the user informed of the progress of the work. Providing feedback in this way enhances the user's perception of the performance of your application and prevents him or her from assuming that nothing is happening. Try to ensure that the user can cancel lengthy operations at any time.

You should also consider using the **Idle** event of the **Application** object to perform simple operations. The **Idle** event provides a simple alternative to using separate threads for background processing. This event fires when the application has no more user interface messages to handle and is about to enter the idle state. You can perform simple operations with this event and take advantage of user inactivity. For example:

[C#]

```
public Form1()
{
InitializeComponent();
Application.Idle += new EventHandler( OnApplicationIdle );
}

private void OnApplicationIdle( object sender, EventArgs e )
{
}
```

[Visual Basic .NET]

```
Public Class Form1
    Inherits System.Windows.Forms.Form

    Public Sub New()
        MyBase.New()

        InitializeComponent()

        AddHandler Application.Idle, AddressOf OnApplicationIdle
    End Sub

    Private Sub OnApplicationIdle(ByVal sender As System.Object, ByVal e As
System.EventArgs)

    End Sub
End Class
```

Note: For more information on using multiple threads in Smart Clients, see Chapter 6, "Using Multiple Threads."

Transaction Guidelines

Transactions can provide essential support for ensuring that business rules are not violated and that data consistency is maintained. A transaction ensures that a set of related tasks either succeed or fail as a unit. You can use transactions to maintain consistency between a local database and other resources, including Message Queuing queues.

For smart client applications that need to work with offline cached data when network connectivity is not available, you should queue the transactional data and synchronize it with the server when network connectivity is available.

You should avoid using distributed transactions involving resources located on the network, as these scenarios may lead to performance problems due to varying network and resource response times. If your application needs to involve a network-located resource in a transaction, you should consider using compensating transactions, which allow your application to cancel a previous request when a local transaction fails. Though compensating transactions may not be suitable for all situations, they allow your application to interact with network resources within the context of a transaction in a loosely coupled manner, reducing the chance that a resource not under the control of the local computer can adversely affect the performance of your application.

Note: For more information on the user of transactions in smart clients, see Chapter 3, "Getting Connected."

Optimizing Application Startup Time

Fast application startup time allows the user to begin interacting with the application almost immediately, giving the user an immediate and favorable perception of your application's performance and usability.

When an application starts, first the CLR is loaded, then your application's main assembly, followed by all of the assemblies that are required to resolve the types of objects referenced from your application's main form. The CLR does *not* load all of the dependent assemblies at this stage; it loads only the assemblies that contain the type definitions for the member variables on your main form class. Once these assemblies are loaded, the just-in-time (JIT) compiler compiles the code for the methods as they are run, starting with the **Main** method. Again, the JIT compiler does *not* compile all of the code in your assembly. Instead, the code is compiled as required on a per method basis.

To minimize the startup time of your application, you should follow these guidelines:

- **Minimize member variables in your application's main form class**. This will minimize the number of types that have to be resolved when the CLR loads the main form class.

- **Minimize the immediate use of types from large base class assemblies, such as the XML libraries or the ADO.NET libraries**. These assemblies take time to load. Using the application configuration classes and the trace switch features will bring in the XML library. Avoid this if application startup time is a priority.

- **Lazy load where possible**. Fetch data only when demanded instead of loading upfront and freezing the UI.

- **Design your applications to use fewer assemblies**. Applications with large numbers of assemblies incur increased performance cost. The cost comes from loading metadata, accessing various memory pages in pre-compiled images in the CLR to load the assembly (if it is precompiled with the Native Image Generator tool, Ngen.exe), JIT compile time, security checks, and so on. You should consider merging assemblies based on their usage patterns to decrease the associated performance cost.

- **Avoid designing monolithic classes that combine the functionality of several components in one**. Factor the design into smaller classes that only need to be compiled when they are actually called.

- **Design your applications to make parallel calls to network services during initialization**. Calls to network services that can run parallel during initialization, can take advantage of asynchronous functionality provided by the service proxies. This helps free the current executing thread and calls services concurrently to get tasks done.

- **Use NGEN.exe to compile and experiment with NGen and non-NGen assemblies, and determine which saves the largest number of working set pages**. NGEN.exe, which ships with the .NET Framework, is used to pre-compile an assembly to create a native image that is then stored in a special part of the global assembly cache, ready for the next time it is required by an application. Creating a native image of an assembly allows the assembly to load and execute faster because the CLR does not need to dynamically generate the code and data structures contained in the assembly. For more information, see the "Working Set Considerations" and "NGen.exe Explained" sections in Chapter 5, "Improving Managed Code Performance" of *Improving. NET Application Performance and Scalability*, at *http://msdn.microsoft.com/library/default.asp?url=/library/en-us/dnpag /html/scalenetchapt05.asp*.

Note: If you use NGEN to pre-compile an assembly, all of its dependent assemblies will be immediately loaded.

Managing Available Resources

The Common Language Runtime (CLR) uses a garbage collector to manage object lifetime and memory usage. This means that objects that are no longer reachable are automatically collected by the garbage collector, with the memory being reclaimed automatically. Objects can be no longer reachable for a number of reasons. For example, there may be no references to the object or all references to the object may be from other objects that can be collected as part of the current collection cycle, While automatic garbage collection frees your code of the burden associated with managing object deletion, it means that your code no longer has explicit control over exactly when an object is deleted.

Consider the following guidelines to ensure that you manage available resources effectively:

- **Ensure that the Dispose method is called when the callee object provides one.** If your code calls objects that support the **Dispose** method, you should ensure you call this method as soon as you finish using the object. Calling the **Dispose** method ensures that unmanaged resources are proactively released instead of waiting until garbage collection occurs. Some objects provide methods in addition to the **Dispose** method that manage resources, such as the **Close** method. In these cases, you should consult the documentation on how to use the additional methods. For example, with the **SqlConnection** object, calling either **Close** or **Dispose** is enough to proactively release the database connection back to the connection pool. One way to ensure that **Dispose** is called as soon as you are done with the object is to use the **using** statement in Visual C# .NET or **Try/Finally** blocks in Visual Basic .NET.

The following code snippets demonstrate the use of **Dispose**.

Example of **using** statement in C#:

```
using( StreamReader myFile = new StreamReader("C:\\ReadMe.Txt")){
string contents = myFile.ReadToEnd();
//... use the contents of the file
} // dispose is called and the StreamReader's resources released
```

Example of **Try/Finally** block in Visual Basic .NET:

```
Dim myFile As StreamReader
myFile = New StreamReader("C:\\ReadMe.Txt")
Try
String contents = myFile.ReadToEnd()
'... use the contents of the file
Finally
myFile.Close()
End Try
```

Note: In C# and C++, **Finalize** methods are implemented as destructors. In Visual Basic .NET, the **Finalize** method is implemented as an override of the **Finalize** subroutine on the **Object** base class.

- **Provide Finalize and Dispose methods if you hold unmanaged resources across client calls**. If you create an object that accesses unmanaged resources in public or protected method calls, then the application needs to control the lifetime of the unmanaged resources. In Figure 8.1, the first case is a call to unmanaged resources where the resource is opened, fetched, and closed. In this case, your object does not need to provide **Finalize** and **Dispose** methods. In the second case, the unmanaged resource is held across method calls; therefore, your object should provide **Finalize** and **Dispose** methods so that the client can explicitly release the resource as soon as the client has finished using the object.

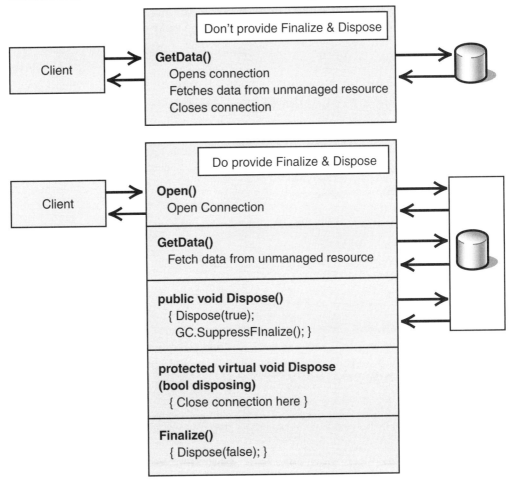

* Simplified View of Dispose Pattern

Figure 8.1
Use of Dispose and Finalize method calls

Garbage collection is generally good for overall performance because it favors speed over memory usage. Objects need to be deleted only when memory resources are low; otherwise, all available application resources are used to the benefit of your application. However, if your object maintains a reference to an unmanaged resource, such as window handle, file, GDI objects, and network connections, then better performance can be achieved if the programmer explicitly releases these resources when they are no longer being used. If you are holding unmanaged resources across client method calls, then the object should allow the caller to explicitly manage resources using the **IDisposable** interface, which provides the **Dispose** method. By implementing **IDisposable**, an object is announcing that it can be asked to clean up deterministically, rather than waiting for garbage collection. The caller of an object that implements **IDisposable** simply calls the **Dispose** method when it has finished with the object so that it can free the resource as appropriate.

For more details on how to implement **IDisposable** on one of your objects, see Chapter 5, "Improving Managed Code Performance," in *Improving .NET Application Performance and Scalability*, at *http://msdn.microsoft.com/library/default.asp?url=/library /en-us/dnpag/html/scalenetchapt05.asp*.

Note: If your disposable object derives from another object that also implements the **IDisposable** interface, you should call the **Dispose** method of the base class to allow it to clean up its resources. You should also call **Dispose** on all objects that are owned by your object that implements the **IDisposable** interface.

The **Finalize** method also allows your object to explicitly release any resources that it has a reference to when the object is being deleted. Due to the non-deterministic nature of the garbage collector, in some cases the **Finalize** method may not be called for a long time. In fact, it may never be called if your application terminates before the object is deleted by the garbage collector. However, it important to use the **Finalize** method as a backup strategy in case the caller doesn't explicitly call the **Dispose** method (both the **Dispose** and **Finalize** methods share the same resource cleanup code). In this way, the resource is likely to be freed at some point, even if this occurs later than is optimal.

Note: To ensure that the cleanup code in **Dispose** and **Finalize** isn't called twice, you should call **GC.SuppressFinalize**, which tells the garbage collector not to call the **Finalize** method.

The garbage collector implements the **Collect** method, which forces the garbage collector to delete all objects pending deletion. This method should not be called from within your application, as the collection cycle runs on a high priority thread. The collection cycle may freeze all the UI threads, resulting in an unresponsive user interface.

For more information, see "Garbage Collection Guidelines," "Finalize and Dispose Guidelines," "Dispose Pattern," and "Finalize and Dispose Guidelines" in *Improving .NET Application Performance and Scalability* at *http://msdn.microsoft.com/library /default.asp?url=/library/en-us/dnpag/html/scalenetchapt05.asp.*

Optimizing Windows Forms Performance

Windows Forms provide a rich user interface for your smart client application and there are a number of techniques you can use to help ensure that Windows Forms provides optimal performance. Before discussing specific techniques, it is useful to review some high-level guidelines that can increase Windows Forms performance substantially.

- **Beware of handle creations**. Windows Forms virtualizes handle creation (that is, it creates and re-creates window handle objects dynamically). Creating handle objects can be expensive; therefore, avoid making unnecessary border style changes or changing MDI parents.

- **Avoid creating applications with very many child controls**. The Microsoft® Windows® operating system has a limit of 10,000 controls per process, but you should avoid having many hundreds of controls on a form as each control consumes memory resources.

The rest of this section discusses more specific techniques you can use to optimize the performance of your application's user interface.

Using BeginUpdate and EndUpdate

A number of Windows Forms controls (for example the **ListView** and **TreeView** controls) implement **BeginUpdate** and **EndUpdate** methods, which suppress repainting of the controls while the underlying data or control properties are manipulated. Using the **BeginUpdate** and **EndUpdate** methods allows you to make significant changes to your controls and avoid having the control repainting itself constantly while those changes are applied. Such repainting leads to a significant performance degradation and a flickering and unresponsive user interface.

For example, if your application has a tree control that requires a large number of node items to be added, you should call **BeginUpdate**, add all of the required node items, and then call **EndUpdate**. The following code example shows a tree control being used to display a hierarchical representation of a number of customers along with their order information.

[C#]

```csharp
// Suppress repainting the TreeView until all the objects have been created.
treeView1.BeginUpdate();

// Clear the TreeView.
treeView1.Nodes.Clear();

// Add a root TreeNode for each Customer object in the ArrayList.
foreach( Customer customer2 in customerArray )
{
    treeView1.Nodes.Add( new TreeNode( customer2.CustomerName ) );

    // Add a child TreeNode for each Order object in the current Customer.
    foreach( Order order1 in customer2.CustomerOrders )
    {
        treeView1.Nodes[ customerArray.IndexOf(customer2) ].Nodes.Add(
            new TreeNode( customer2.CustomerName + "." + order1.OrderID ) );
    }
}

// Begin repainting the TreeView.
treeView1.EndUpdate();
```

[Visual Basic .NET]

```vbnet
    ' Suppress repainting the TreeView until all the objects have been created.
    TreeView1.BeginUpdate()

' Clear the TreeView
TreeView1.Nodes.Clear()

' Add a root TreeNode for each Customer object in the ArrayList
For Each customer2 As Customer In customerArray
    TreeView1.Nodes.Add(New TreeNode(customer2.CustomerName))

    ' Add a child TreeNode for each Order object in the current Customer.
    For Each order1 As Order In customer2.CustomerOrders
        TreeView1.Nodes(Array.IndexOf(customerArray, customer2)).Nodes.Add( _
                New TreeNode(customer2.CustomerName & "." & order1.OrderID))
    Next
Next

' Begin repainting the TreeView.
TreeView1.EndUpdate()
```

You should use the **BeginUpdate** and **EndUpdate** methods even when you do not expect many objects to be added to the control. In most cases, you will not be aware of the exact number of items to be added until runtime. Therefore, to cope elegantly with an unusually large amount of data and for future requirements, you should always call the **BeginUpdate** and **EndUpdate** methods.

Note: Calling the **AddRange** method of many of the **Collection** classes used by Windows Forms controls will automatically call **BeginUpdate** and **EndUpdate** for you.

Using SuspendLayout and ResumeLayout

A number of Windows Forms controls (for example the **ListView** and **TreeView** controls) implement **SuspendLayout** and **ResumeLayout** methods, which prevent the control from creating multiple layout events while the child controls are being added.

If your controls programmatically add and remove child controls or perform dynamic layout, then you should call the **SuspendLayout** and **ResumeLayout** methods. The **SuspendLayout** method allows multiple actions to be performed on a control without having to perform a layout for each change. For example, if you resize and move a control, each operation would raise a separate layout event.

These methods operate in a similar manner to the **BeginUpdate** and **EndUpdate** methods and provide the same benefits in terms of performance and user interface stability.

The example below programmatically adds buttons to the parent form:

[C#]
```csharp
private void AddButtons()
{
  // Suspend the form layout and add two buttons.
  this.SuspendLayout();
  Button buttonOK = new Button();
  buttonOK.Location = new Point(10, 10);
  buttonOK.Size = new Size(75, 25);
  buttonOK.Text = "OK";

  Button buttonCancel = new Button();
  buttonCancel.Location = new Point(90, 10);
  buttonCancel.Size = new Size(75, 25);
  buttonCancel.Text = "Cancel";

  this.Controls.AddRange(new Control[]{buttonOK, buttonCancel});
  this.ResumeLayout();
}
```

[Visual Basic .NET]

```
Private Sub AddButtons()
        ' Suspend the form layout and add two buttons
        Me.SuspendLayout()
        Dim buttonOK As New Button
        buttonOK.Location = New Point(10, 10)
        buttonOK.Size = New Size(75, 25)
        buttonOK.Text = "OK"

        Dim buttonCancel As New Button
        buttonCancel.Location = New Point(90, 10)
        buttonCancel.Size = New Size(75, 25)
        buttonCancel.Text = "Cancel"

        Me.Controls.AddRange(New Control() { buttonOK, buttonCancel } )
        Me.ResumeLayout()
End Sub
```

You should use the **SuspendLayout** and **ResumeLayout** methods whenever you add or remove controls, perform dynamic layout of the child controls, or set any properties that affect the layout of the control, such as the size, location, anchor, or dock properties.

Handling Images

If your application displays a large number of image files, such as .jpg and .gif files, then you can improve display performance significantly by pre-rendering the images into a bitmap format.

To use this technique, first load the image from file and then render to a bitmap using the PARGB format. The following code sample loads a file from disk and then uses the class to render the image into a pre-multiplied, alpha-blended RGB format. For example:

[C#]

```
if ( image != null && image is Bitmap )
{
Bitmap bm = (Bitmap)image;
Bitmap newImage = new Bitmap( bm.Width, bm.Height,
    System.Drawing.Imaging.PixelFormat.Format32bppPArgb );
using ( Graphics g = Graphics.FromImage( newImage ) )
{
g.DrawImage( bm, new Rectangle( 0,0, bm.Width, bm.Height ) );
}
image = newImage;
}
```

[Visual Basic .NET]

```
If Not(image Is Nothing)  AndAlso (TypeOf image Is Bitmap) Then
    Dim bm As Bitmap = CType(image, Bitmap)
    Dim newImage As New Bitmap(bm.Width, bm.Height, _
        System.Drawing.Imaging.PixelFormat.Format32bppPArgb)


    Using g As Graphics = Graphics.FromImage(newImage)
        g.DrawImage(bm, New Rectangle(0, 0, bm.Width, bm.Height))
    End Using

    image = newImage
End If
```

Use Paging and Lazy Loading

In most cases, you should retrieve or display data only when it is needed. If your application needs to retrieve and display a lot of information, you should consider breaking the data into pages and displaying the data one page at a time. This allows your user interface to perform better because it does not have to display a large amount of data. In addition, this can improve the usability of your application because the user is not confronted with an abundance of data at once and can navigate more easily to find the exact data he or she needs.

For example, if your application displays product data from a large product catalog, you could display the items in alphabetical order with all the products beginning with "A" displayed on one page and all the products beginning with "B" on the next page. You could then allow the user to navigate directly to the appropriate page so that he or she does not need to scroll through all of the pages to reach the data he or she needs.

Paging the data in this way can also allow you to fetch the data in the background as it is required. For instance, you might only need to fetch the first page of information to display and allow the user to interact with. You can then fetch the next page of data in the background ready for when the user needs it. This technique can be particularly effective when combined with data caching.

You can also increase the performance of your smart client application by using lazy loading techniques. Instead of immediately loading data or resources that you might need at some point in the future, you load them as they are needed. You can use lazy loading to increase the performance of your user interface when constructing large lists or tree structures. In this case, you can load the data when the user needs to see it, for example when a tree node is expanded.

Optimizing Display Speed

You can optimize your application's display speed in a number of different ways, according to the techniques you are using to display the user interface controls and application forms.

When your application starts, you should consider displaying as simple a user interface as possible. This will decrease startup time and present an uncluttered and easy to use user-interface to the user. Also, you should try to avoid referencing classes and loading any data at startup that is not immediately required. This will improve the application and .NET framework initialization time and improve the display speed of the application.

When you need to display a dialog box or form, you should keep them hidden until they are ready to be displayed, to reduce the amount of painting necessary. This will help to ensure that the form is only displayed once it has been initialized.

If your application has controls that contain child controls covering the entire client surface area, you should consider setting the control background style to opaque. This avoid redrawing the control's background on every paint event. You can set the control's style by using the **SetStyle** method. Use **ControlsStyles.Opaque** enumeration to specify an opaque control style.

You should avoid any unnecessary repainting of controls. One approach is to hide controls while you are setting their properties. Applications that have complex drawing code in the **OnPaint** event are able to redraw just the invalidated region of the form, instead of painting the entire form. The **PaintEventArgs** parameter of the **OnPaint** event contains a **ClipRect** structure that indicates which part of the window is invalidated. This reduces the time that the user waits to see a completed display.

Use standard drawing optimization, such as clipping, double buffering, and **ClipRectangle**. This will also help improve the display performance of your smart client application by preventing unnecessary drawing operations for portions of the display that are not visible or that require redrawing. For more information on enhancing painting performance, see *Painting techniques using Windows Forms for the Microsoft .NET Framework* at *http://windowsforms.net/articles/windowsformspainting.aspx*.

If your display includes animation or changes a display element often, you should use double or multiple buffering to prepare the next image while the current one is being painted. The **ControlStyles** enumeration in the **System.Windows.Forms** namespace applies to many controls, and the **DoubleBuffer** member can help prevent flickering. Turning on the **DoubleBuffer** style will cause your controls painting to be done to an off-screen buffer and then painted all at once to the screen. While this helps prevent flickering, it does use more memory for the allocated buffer.

Performance Tuning and Diagnosis

Tackling performance issues at the design and implementation stages is the most cost effective way to meet your application's performance goals. However, you can only be truly effective in optimizing the performance of your applications if you test your application's performance often and as early in the development phase as possible.

While designing and testing for performance are both important, optimizing every component and all of the code at these early stages is not an efficient use of resources, and so should be avoided. Consequently, your application may suffer from unexpected performance problems that you did not anticipate at the design stage. For example, you may experience performance problems due to the unforeseen interaction between two systems or components, or you may use pre-existing code that does not perform as hoped. In this case, you need to track down the source of the performance problem so that you can address it appropriately.

This section discusses a number of tools and techniques that will help you diagnose performance issues, and tune your application for optimum performance.

Setting Performance Goals

As you design and architect your smart client application, you should carefully consider the requirements in terms of performance, and define suitable performance goals. When defining these goals, consider how you are going to measure the application's actual performance. Your performance metrics should clearly represent the important performance characteristics of the application. Try to avoid ambiguous or incomplete goals that cannot be accurately measured, such as "the application must run fast" or "the application must load quickly." You need to know the performance and scalability goals of your application so that you can design to meet them and plan your tests around them. Be sure that your goals are measurable and verifiable.

Well-defined performance metrics allow you to track the performance of your application accurately so that you can determine whether the application meets its performance goals or not. These metrics should be included in your application's test plan, so that they can be measured during the testing phase of your application.

This section focuses on the definition of specific performance goals relevant to a smart client application. If you are also designing and building the network services that the client application will consume, you need to define appropriate performance goals for these as well. In this case, you should be sure to consider the performance requirements of the system as a whole and how the performance of each part of the application relates to the other parts and to the system in its entirety.

Considering the User's Perspective

As you determine suitable performance goals for a smart client application, you should carefully consider the perspective of the user. For a smart client application, performance is related to usability and user perception. For example, a lengthy operation could be acceptable to the user as long as that user is able to keep working and is provided with adequate feedback on progress of the operation.

When determining requirements, it is often useful to break an application's functionality into a number of usage scenarios or use cases. You should identify the use cases and scenarios that are critical and required to meet specific performance objectives. Tasks that are common to many use cases and that are performed often should be designed to perform well. Similarly, tasks that demand the user's complete attention and from which they can't switch to perform other tasks need to provide an optimized and efficient user experience. Tasks that are not used very often or that do not stop the user from performing other tasks may not need to be highly tuned.

For each performance-sensitive task that you identify, you should precisely define what the user does and how the application responds. You should also determine which network and client resources or components each task uses. This information will influence the performance goals and will drive the tests that measure performance.

Usability studies provide a very valuable source of information and can greatly influence the definition of performance goals. A formal usability study can be very helpful in determining how users perform their work, which usage scenarios are common and which are not, what tasks the users perform often, and what characteristics of the application are important from a performance perspective. If you are building a new application, you should consider providing a prototype or mock-up of the application to allow rudimentary usability testing to be carried out.

Considering the Application Operating Environment

It is important to evaluate the environment in which your application will be operating, as this may impose constraints on your application that must be reflected in the performance goals you set.

Network-located services may impose performance constraints on your application. For example, you may be required to interact with a Web service over which you have no control. In such cases, it is important to determine the performance of the service and to determine whether this will have an effect on the performance of your client application.

You should also determine how the performance of any dependent services and components may vary with time. Some systems experience fairly constant usage while other experience wildly fluctuating usage at certain times of the day or week. These differences could adversely affect the performance of your application at critical times. For example, a service that provides application deployment and update services may be slow to respond on Monday morning at 9:00 AM as all users upgrade to the latest version of an application.

It is also important to accurately model the performance of all dependent systems and components, so that your application can be tested in an environment that closely mimics the real environment in which it will be deployed. For each system, you should determine the performance profile and the minimum, average, and peak performance characteristics. You can then use this data as appropriate when defining the performance requirements for your application.

You should also carefully consider the hardware on which your application will run. You will need to determine the target hardware configuration, in terms of processor, memory, graphics capability, and so on — or at least a minimum configuration below which you cannot guarantee performance.

Often the business environment in which your application will operate will dictate some of the more exacting performance requirements. For example, an application that executes real-time stock trading will be required to execute these trades and display all of the relevant data in a timely manner.

Performance Tuning Process

Performance tuning your application is an iterative process. This process consists of a number of stages that are repeated until the application meets its performance goals. (See Figure 8.2.)

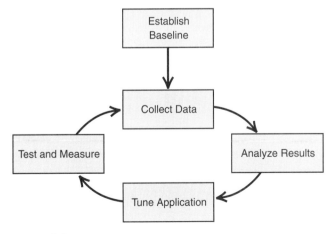

Figure 8.2
Performance tuning process

As Figure 8.2 illustrates, performance tuning requires that you complete the following processes:

- **Establish Baseline**. Before you begin tuning your application for performance, you must have a well-defined baseline for the performance goals, objectives, and metrics. This could include specifics such as application working set size, time to load data (for example, a catalogue), transaction duration, and so on.

- **Collect Data**. You will need to gauge your application's performance by measuring it against the performance goals that you have defined. Performance goals should embody specific and measurable metrics that allow you to quantify your application's performance at any point in time. To allow you to collect performance data, you may have to instrument your application so that the required performance data can be published and collected. Some of the options that you have to accomplish this are discussed in detail in the next section.

- **Analyze Results**. After you have collected your application's performance data, you will be able to prioritize your performance tuning effort by determining which application features require the most attention. In addition, you can use this data to determine where any performance bottlenecks are. Often, you will only be able to determine the exact location of the bottleneck by gathering more detailed performance data: for example, by using application instrumentation. Performance profiling tools may help you to identify the bottleneck.

- **Tune Application**. After you have identified a bottleneck, you will probably need to modify the application or its configuration to try and solve the problem. You should aim to minimize changes so that you can determine the effect of the changes on the application's performance. If you make more than one change at the same time, it can be difficult to determine what effect each change had on the application's overall performance.

- **Test and Measure**. After you have changed your application or its configuration, you should test it again to determine what effect your changes have and to allow new performance data to be gathered. Performance work often requires architectural or other high-impact changes so thorough testing is critical. Your application's test plan should exercise the full range of functionality that your application implements, for all anticipated scenarios and on client machines configured with the appropriate hardware and software. If your application uses network resources, you should load these resources so that you can gain accurate measurements for how your application performs in such an environment.

The above process will allow you to focus on specific performance problems by measuring your applications overall performance against specific goals.

Performance Tools

There are number of tools available to you which can help you to collect and analyze your application's performance data. Each of the tools described in this section have different functionality that you can use to measure, analyze, and find performance bottlenecks in your application.

Note: In addition to the tools described here, there are a number of other options and third-party tools available. For a description of other logging and exception management options, see the *Exception Management Architecture Guide*, at *http://msdn.microsoft.com/library/default.asp?url= /library/en-us/dnbda/html/exceptdotnet.asp*.

You should carefully consider your exact requirements before deciding on which tools are most appropriate to your needs.

Using Performance Logs and Alerts

Performance Logs and Alerts is an administrative performance monitoring tool that ships as part of the Windows operating system. It relies on performance counters that are published by the various Windows components, subsystems, and applications to allow you to track resource usage and to plot them graphically against time.

You can use Performance Logs and Alerts to monitor standard performance counters, such as memory usage or processor usage, or you can define your own custom counters to monitor application-specific activity.

The .NET CLR provides a number of useful performance counters that can give you insight into how well your application is performing. Some of the more relevant performance objects are:

- **.NET CLR Memory**. Provides data on the memory usage of a managed .NET application, including the amount of memory that your application is using and the time spent garbage collecting unused objects.

- **.NET CLR Loading**. Provides data on the number of classes and application domains that your application is using and the rate at which they are being loaded and unloaded.

- **.NET CLR Locks and Threads**. Provides performance data related to the threads used within your application, including the number of threads and the rate of contention between threads trying to get simultaneous access to a protected resource.

- **.NET CLR Networking**. Provides performance counters that relate to sending and receiving data over the network, including the number of bytes sent and received per second and the number of active connections.

- **.NET CLR Exceptions**. Provides reports on the number of exceptions being thrown and caught by your application.

To learn more about these counters, their thresholds, what to measure and how to measure them see the section, "CLR and Managed Code" in Chapter 15, "Measuring .NET Application Performance" of *Improving .NET Application Performance and Scalability*, at *http://msdn.microsoft.com/library/default.asp?url=/library/en-us/dnpag/html /scalenetchapt15.asp*.

Your application can also provide application-specific performance counters that you can easily monitor by using Performance Logs and Alerts. You can define a custom performance counter as shown in the following example:

[C#]

```
PerformanceCounter counter = new PerformanceCounter( "Category",
        "CounterName", false );
```

[Visual Basic .NET]

```
Dim counter As New PerformanceCounter("Category", "CounterName", False)
```

Once the performance counter object is created, you can specify a category for your custom performance counters and keep all related counters together. The **PerformanceCounter** class is defined in the **System.Diagnostics** namespace, along with a number of other classes that you can use to read and define performance counters and categories. For more information on creating custom performance counters see, Knowledge Base article 317679, "How to create and make changes to a custom counter for the Windows Performance Monitor by using Visual Basic .NET," at *http://support.microsoft.com/default.aspx?scid=kb;en-us;317679*.

Note: To register a performance counter, you must first register the category. You must have sufficient permissions to register a performance counter category, which may affect how you need to deploy your application.

Instrumentation

There are a number of tools and technologies you can use to help instrument your application and generate information needed to measure the application performance. These tools and technologies include:

- **Event Tracing for Windows (ETW)**. This ETW subsystem provides a low system overhead (as compared to Performance Logs and Alerts) means of monitoring performance of a system under load. This is primarily for server applications that must frequently log events, errors, warnings, or audits. For more information, see "Event Tracing" in the Microsoft Platform SDK at *http://msdn.microsoft.com/library /default.asp?url=/library/en-us/perfmon/base/event_tracing.asp*.

- **Enterprise Instrumentation Framework (EIF)**. The EIF is an extensible and configurable framework that you can use to instrument your smart client application. It provides an extensible event schema and unified API that uses existing events, logging, and tracing mechanisms built into Windows, including the Windows Management Instrumentation (WMI), the Windows Event Log, and Windows Event Tracing. It greatly simplifies the coding required to publish application events. If you are planning to use EIF, you need to install EIF on the client computer by using the EIF .msi. If you want to use the EIF in your smart client application, you need to consider this requirement when you decide how to deploy your application. For more information, see "How To: Use EIF" at *http://msdn.microsoft.com/library/default.asp?url=/library/en-us/dnpag/html /scalenethowto14.asp*.

- **Logging Application Block**. The Logging Application Block provides extensible and reusable code components to help you produce instrumented applications. It builds on capabilities of the EIF to provide functionalities such as enhancements to the event schema, multiple log levels, additional event sinks, and so on. For more information, see the "Logging Application Block" at *http://msdn.microsoft.com /library/default.asp?url=/library/en-us/dnpag/html/Logging.asp*.

- **Windows Management Instrumentation (WMI)**. The WMI component is part of the Windows operating system and provides programming interfaces for accessing management information and control in an enterprise. This is most commonly used by system administrators to automate administration tasks using scripts that invoke the WMI component. For more information, see Windows Management Instrumentation at *http://msdn.microsoft.com/library/default.asp?url= /library/en-us/wmisdk/wmi/wmi_start_page.asp*.

- **Debug and Trace Classes**. The .NET framework provides **Debug** and **Trace** classes under the **System.Diagnosis** to instrument your code. The **Debug** class is primarily used for printing debug information and checking for assertions. The **Trace** class allows you to instrument release builds to monitor the health of your application at run time. In Visual Studio .NET, tracing is enabled by default. When using the command-line build you must add the **/d:Trace** flag for the compiler or **#define TRACE** in the your Visual C# .NET source code to enable tracing. For Visual Basic .NET source code, you must add **/d:TRACE=True** for the command-line compiler. For more information, see Knowledge Base article 815788, "HOW TO: Trace and Debug in Visual C# .NET," at *http://support.microsoft.com /default.aspx?scid=kb;en-us;815788*.

CLR Profiler

The CLR Profiler is a memory profiling tool provided by Microsoft and available for download from MSDN. It enables you to look at the managed heap of your application's process and investigate the behavior of the garbage collector. Using this tool, you can obtain useful information about the execution, memory allocation, and memory consumption of your application. This information can help you understand how your application is using memory and how you can optimize your application's memory use.

The CLR Profiler is available at *http://msdn.microsoft.com/netframework/downloads/tools /default.aspx*. Also see "How to use CLR Profiler" at *http://msdn.microsoft.com/library /default.asp?url=/library/en-us/dnpag/html/scalenethowto13.asp?frame=true* for details on how to use the CLR Profiler tool.

The CLR Profiler logs memory consumption and garbage collector behavior information in a log file. You can then analyze this data with the CLR Profiler by using number of different graphical views. Some of the more important views are:

- **Allocation Graph**. Shows the call stack for how objects were allocated. You can use this view to see the cost of each allocation by method, isolate allocations that you were not expecting, and view possible excessive allocations by a method.

- **Assembly, Module, Function, and Class Graph**. Shows which methods caused the loading of which assemblies, functions, modules, or classes.

- **Call Graph**. Lets you see which methods call which other methods and how frequently. You can use this graph to determine the cost of library calls and which methods are called or how many calls are made to a specific method.

- **Time Line**. Provides a text-based, chronological, hierarchical view of your application's execution. Use this view to see what types are allocated and their size. You can also use this view to see which assemblies are loaded as result of method calls and to analyze allocations that you were not expecting. You can analyze the use of finalizers and to identify methods where **Close** or **Dispose** have not been implemented or called, thereby causing bottlenecks.

You can use CLR Profiler.exe to identify and isolate problems related to garbage collection. These include memory consumption issues such as excessive or unknown allocations, memory leaks, long-lived objects, and the percentage of time spent performing garbage collection.

Note: For more detailed information on how to use the CLR Profiler tool, see "Improving .NET Application Performance and Scalability" at *http://msdn.microsoft.com/library/default.asp?url= /library/en-us/dnpag/html/scalenethowto13.asp?frame=true.*

Summary

To fully realize the potential of a smart client application, you need to carefully consider performance issues during the application's design phase. By addressing these issues at an early stage, you can contain costs during the application design process and reduce the likelihood of running into performance problems late in the development cycle.

This chapter examined different techniques that you can use as you architect and design your smart client applications to ensure that you optimize their performance. It has also looked at a number of tools and techniques you can use to determine performance problems within your smart client applications.

References

For more information, see the following:

- *http://msdn.microsoft.com/perf*
- *http://www.windowsforms.net/Default.aspx*
- *http://msdn.microsoft.com/vstudio/using/understand/perf/*
- *http://msdn.microsoft.com/library/default.asp?url=/library/en-us/dnnetcomp/html /netcfimproveformloadperf.asp*
- *http://msdn.microsoft.com/library/default.asp?url=/library/en-us/dndotnet/html /highperfmanagedapps.asp*
- *http://msdn.microsoft.com/msdnmag/issues/02/08/AdvancedBasics/default.aspx*
- *http://msdn.microsoft.com/library/default.asp?url=/msdnmag/issues/04/01/NET /toc.asp?frame=true*
- *http://msdn.microsoft.com/library/default.asp?url=/msdnmag/issues/03/02 /Multithreading/toc.asp?frame=true*

Collaborators and Reviewers

- **Special thanks to our reviewers**: Mark Boulter, Jamie Cool, Keith Yedlin, Richard Turner; Ivan Medvedev; Ram Singh, Philip Vaughn; Jay Schmelzer, Nathan Blecharczyk; Andy Dunn, Devendra Tiwari, Eric Leonard, Ken Perilman, Per Vonge Nielsen, Naveen Yajaman, and Chris Sells, Microsoft Corporation
- **Special thanks to our external reviewer**: Steven John Pack, Avanade
- **Thanks to our editors and production team for helping to ensure a quality experience for the reader**: Sharon Smith, Microsoft; Susan Filkins, Entirenet; and Tina Burden McGrayne, Entirenet; and Sanjeev Garg, Satyam Computer Services
- **Thanks to our test team**: Prashant Bansode and Guru Shankar Sundaram, InfoSys Technologies Limited
- **Thanks to our product management**: Eugenio Pace, Microsoft; and Vasu Vijay, Electronic Data Systems

Index

patterns & practices

About Microsoft *patterns & practices*

Microsoft *patterns & practices* guides contain specific recommendations illustrating how to design, build, deploy, and operate architecturally sound solutions to challenging business and technical scenarios. They offer deep technical guidance based on real-world experience that goes far beyond white papers to help enterprise IT professionals, information workers, and developers quickly deliver sound solutions.

IT Professionals, information workers, and developers can choose from four types of *patterns & practices*:

- **Patterns**—Patterns are a consistent way of documenting solutions to commonly occurring problems. Patterns are available that address specific architecture, design, and implementation problems. Each pattern also has an associated GotDotNet Community.

- **Reference Architectures**—Reference Architectures are IT system-level architectures that address the business requirements, LifeCycle requirements, and technical constraints for commonly occurring scenarios. Reference Architectures focus on planning the architecture of IT systems.

- **Reference Building Blocks and IT Services**—References Building Blocks and IT Services are re-usable sub-system designs that address common technical challenges across a wide range of scenarios. Many include tested reference implementations to accelerate development. Reference Building Blocks and IT Services focus on the design and implementation of sub-systems.

- **Lifecycle Practices**—Lifecycle Practices provide guidance for tasks outside the scope of architecture and design such as deployment and operations in a production environment.

Patterns & practices guides are reviewed and approved by Microsoft engineering teams, consultants, Product Support Services, and by partners and customers. *Patterns & practices* guides are:

- **Proven**—They are based on field experience.
- **Authoritative**—They offer the best advice available.
- **Accurate**—They are technically validated and tested.
- **Actionable**—They provide the steps to success.
- **Relevant**—They address real-world problems based on customer scenarios.

Patterns & practices guides are designed to help IT professionals, information workers, and developers:

Reduce project cost

- Exploit the Microsoft engineering efforts to save time and money on your projects.
- Follow the Microsoft recommendations to lower your project risk and achieve predictable outcomes.

Increase confidence in solutions

- Build your solutions on proven Microsoft recommendations so you can have total confidence in your results.
- Rely on thoroughly tested and supported guidance, but production quality recommendations and code, not just samples.

Deliver strategic IT advantage

- Solve your problems today and take advantage of future Microsoft technologies with practical advice.

To learn more about *patterns & practices* visit: **http://msdn.microsoft.com/practices**
To purchase *patterns & practices* guides visit: **http://shop.microsoft.com/practices**

patterns & practices: Current Titles

October 2003

Title	Link to Online Version	Book
Patterns		
Enterprise Solution Patterns using Microsoft .NET	*http://msdn.microsoft.com/practices/type/Patterns /Enterprise/default.asp*	▣
Microsoft Data Patterns	*http://msdn.microsoft.com/practices/type/Patterns /Data/default.asp*	
Reference Architectures		
Application Architecture for .NET: Designing Applications and Services	*http://msdn.microsoft.com/library/default.asp?url= /library/en-us/dnbda/html/distapp.asp*	▣
Enterprise Notification Reference Architecture for Exchange 2000 Server	*http://msdn.microsoft.com/library/default.asp?url= /library/en-us/dnentdevgen/html/enraelp.asp*	
Improving Web Application Security: Threats and Countermeasures	*http://msdn.microsoft.com/library/default.asp?url= /library/en-us/dnnetsec/html/ThreatCounter.asp*	▣
Microsoft Accelerator for Six Sigma	*http://www.microsoft.com/technet/treeview /default.asp?url=/technet/itsolutions/mso/sixsigma /default.asp*	
Microsoft Active Directory Branch Office Guide: Volume 1: Planning	*http://www.microsoft.com/technet/treeview /default.asp?url=/technet/prodtechnol/ad /windows2000/deploy/adguide/default.asp*	▣
Microsoft Active Directory Branch Office Series Volume 2: Deployment and Operations	*http://www.microsoft.com/technet/treeview /default.asp?url=/technet/prodtechnol/ad /windows2000/deploy/adguide/default.asp*	▣
Microsoft Content Integration Pack for Content Management Server 2001 and SharePoint Portal Server 2001	*http://msdn.microsoft.com/library/default.asp?url= /library/en-us/dncip/html/cip.asp*	
Microsoft Exchange 2000 Server Hosting Series Volume 1: Planning	Online Version not available	▣
Microsoft Exchange 2000 Server Hosting Series Volume 2: Deployment	Online Version not available	▣

Title	Link to Online Version	Book
Microsoft Exchange 2000 Server Upgrade Series Volume 1: Planning	*http://www.microsoft.com/technet/treeview /default.asp?url=/technet/itsolutions/guide /default.asp*	▦
Microsoft Exchange 2000 Server Upgrade Series Volume 2: Deployment	*http://www.microsoft.com/technet/treeview /default.asp?url=/technet/itsolutions/guide /default.asp*	▦
Microsoft Solution for Intranets	*http://www.microsoft.com/technet/treeview /default.asp?url=/technet/itsolutions/mso /msi/Default.asp*	
Microsoft Solution for Securing Wireless LANs	*http://www.microsoft.com/downloads /details.aspx?FamilyId=CDB639B3-010B-47E7-B23 4-A27CDA291DAD&displaylang=en*	
Microsoft Systems Architecture— Enterprise Data Center	*http://www.microsoft.com/technet/treeview /default.asp?url=/technet/itsolutions/edc /Default.asp*	
Microsoft Systems Architecture— Internet Data Center	*http://www.microsoft.com/technet/treeview/ default.asp?url=/technet/itsolutions/idc/default.asp*	
The Enterprise Project Management Solution	*http://www.microsoft.com/technet/treeview /default.asp?url=/technet/itsolutions/mso/epm /default.asp*	
UNIX Application Migration Guide	*http://msdn.microsoft.com/library/default.asp?url= /library/en-us/dnucmg/html/ucmglp.asp*	▦
Reference Building Blocks and IT Services		
.NET Data Access Architecture Guide	*http://msdn.microsoft.com/library/default.asp?url= /library/en-us/dnbda/html/daag.asp*	
Application Updater Application Block	*http://msdn.microsoft.com/library/default.asp?url= /library/en-us/dnbda/html/updater.asp*	
Asynchronous Invocation Application Block	*http://msdn.microsoft.com/library/default.asp?url= /library/en-us/dnpag/html/paiblock.asp*	
Authentication in ASP.NET: .NET Security Guidance	*http://msdn.microsoft.com/library/default.asp?url= /library/en-us/dnbda/html/authaspdotnet.asp*	
Building Interoperable Web Services: WS-I Basic Profile 1.0	*http://msdn.microsoft.com/library/default.asp?url= /library/en-us/dnsvcinter/html/wsi-bp_msdn_ landingpage.asp*	▦
Building Secure ASP.NET Applications: Authentication, Authorization, and Secure Communication	*http://msdn.microsoft.com/library/default.asp?url= /library/en-us/dnnetsec/html/secnetlpMSDN.asp*	▦

Title	Link to Online Version	Book
Caching Application Block	http://msdn.microsoft.com/library/default.asp?url= /library/en-us/dnpag/html/Cachingblock.asp	
Caching Architecture Guide for .Net Framework Applications	http://msdn.microsoft.com/library/default.asp?url= /library/en-us/dnbda/html/CachingArch.asp?frame= true	
Configuration Management Application Block	http://msdn.microsoft.com/library/default.asp?url= /library/en-us/dnbda/html/cmab.asp	
Data Access Application Block for .NET	http://msdn.microsoft.com/library/default.asp?url= /library/en-us/dnbda/html/daab-rm.asp	
Designing Application-Managed Authorization	http://msdn.microsoft.com/library/?url=/library /en-us/dnbda/html/damaz.asp	
Designing Data Tier Components and Passing Data Through Tiers	http://msdn.microsoft.com/library/default.asp?url= /library/en-us/dnbda/html/BOAGag.asp	
Exception Management Application Block for .NET	http://msdn.microsoft.com/library/default.asp?url= /library/en-us/dnbda/html/emab-rm.asp	
Exception Management Architecture Guide	http://msdn.microsoft.com/library/default.asp?url= /library/en-us/dnbda/html/exceptdotnet.asp	
Microsoft .NET/COM Migration and Interoperability	http://msdn.microsoft.com/library/default.asp?url= /library/en-us/dnbda/html/cominterop.asp	
Microsoft Windows Server 2003 Security Guide	http://www.microsoft.com/downloads/ details.aspx?FamilyId=8A2643C1-0685-4D89-B655- 521EA6C7B4DB&displaylang=en	
Monitoring in .NET Distributed Application Design	http://msdn.microsoft.com/library/default.asp?url= /library/en-us/dnbda/html/monitordotnet.asp	
New Application Installation using Systems Management Server	http://www.microsoft.com/business/reducecosts /efficiency/manageability/application.mspx	
Patch Management using Microsoft Systems Management Server - Operations Guide	http://www.microsoft.com/technet/treeview/ default.asp?url=/technet/itsolutions/msm/swdist/ pmsms/pmsmsog.asp	
Patch Management Using Microsoft Software Update Services - Operations Guide	http://www.microsoft.com/technet/treeview/ default.asp?url=/technet/itsolutions/msm/swdist/ pmsus/pmsusog.asp	
Service Aggregation Application Block	http://msdn.microsoft.com/library/default.asp?url= /library/en-us/dnpag/html/serviceagg.asp	
Service Monitoring and Control using Microsoft Operations Manager	http://www.microsoft.com/business/reducecosts /efficiency/manageability/monitoring.mspx	

Title	Link to Online Version	Book
User Interface Process Application Block	http://msdn.microsoft.com/library/default.asp?url=/library/en-us/dnbda/html/uip.asp	
Web Service Façade for Legacy Applications	http://msdn.microsoft.com/library/default.asp?url=/library/en-us/dnpag/html/wsfacadelegacyapp.asp	
Lifecycle Practices		
Backup and Restore for Internet Data Center	http://www.microsoft.com/technet/treeview/default.asp?url=/technet/ittasks/maintain/backuprest/Default.asp	
Deploying .NET Applications: Lifecycle Guide	http://msdn.microsoft.com/library/default.asp?url=/library/en-us/dnbda/html/DALGRoadmap.asp	
Microsoft Exchange 2000 Server Operations Guide	http://www.microsoft.com/technet/treeview/default.asp?url=/technet/prodtechnol/exchange/exchange2000/maintain/operate/opsguide/default.asp	
Microsoft SQL Server 2000 High Availability Series: Volume 1: Planning	http://www.microsoft.com/technet/treeview/default.asp?url=/technet/prodtechnol/sql/deploy/confeat/sqlha/SQLHALP.asp	
Microsoft SQL Server 2000 High Availability Series: Volume 2: Deployment	http://www.microsoft.com/technet/treeview/default.asp?url=/technet/prodtechnol/sql/deploy/confeat/sqlha/SQLHALP.asp	
Microsoft SQL Server 2000 Operations Guide	http://www.microsoft.com/technet/treeview/default.asp?url=/technet/prodtechnol/sql/maintain/operate/opsguide/default.asp	
Operating .NET-Based Applications	http://www.microsoft.com/technet/treeview/default.asp?url=/technet/itsolutions/net/maintain/opnetapp/default.asp	
Production Debugging for .NET-Connected Applications	http://msdn.microsoft.com/library/default.asp?url=/library/en-us/dnbda/html/DBGrm.asp	
Security Operations for Microsoft Windows 2000 Server	http://www.microsoft.com/technet/treeview/default.asp?url=/technet/security/prodtech/win2000/secwin2k/default.asp	
Security Operations Guide for Exchange 2000 Server	http://www.microsoft.com/technet/treeview/default.asp?url=/technet/security/prodtech/mailexch/opsguide/default.asp	
Team Development with Visual Studio .NET and Visual SourceSafe	http://msdn.microsoft.com/library/default.asp?url=/library/en-us/dnbda/html/tdlg_rm.asp	

 This title is available as a Book